GW00786405

London 28/...

PRACTICE TESTS FOR CAMBRIDGE CE

PROFICIENCY

— IN ENGLISH —

NEW SYLLABUS

SET ONE

MARGARET ARCHER ENID NOLAN-WOODS

Nelson

Thomas Nelson and Sons Ltd
Nelson House   Mayfield Road
Walton-on-Thames   Surrey KT12 5PL

51 York Place
Edinburgh EH1 3JD

Yi Xiu Factory Building
Unit 05-06   5th Floor
65 Sims Avenue   Singapore 1438

Thomas Nelson (Hong Kong) Ltd
Toppan Building 10/F
22A Westlands Road
Quarry Bay   Hong Kong

Thomas Nelson (Kenya) Ltd
P.O. Box 18123
Nairobi   Kenya

© M. Archer and E. Nolan-Woods 1983

First published by Thomas Nelson and Sons Ltd 1984
Reprinted 1984, 1985

ISBN 0-17-555519-2

NCN 71-ECE-9166-03

All Rights Reserved. This publication is protected in the United
Kingdom by the Copyright Act 1956 and in other countries by
comparable legislation. No part of it may be reproduced or recorded by
any means without the permission of the publisher. This prohibition
extends (with certain very limited exceptions) to photocopying and
similar processes, and written permission to make a copy or copies must
therefore be obtained from the publisher in advance. It is advisable to
consult the publisher if there is any doubt regarding the legality of any
proposed copying.

Printed and bound in Hong Kong

ACKNOWLEDGEMENTS

Thanks are due to the following for permission to reproduce copyright material:

Paul Theroux for an extract from *The Old Patagonian Express*; The Institution of Environmental Health Officers for their information leaflet on the water emergency; Robin Kerrod and Octopus Books Limited for the passages on ballons and airships and Neanderthal man from *The Way it Works*; Pinelog Products Limited for an extract from their advertisement for Pinelog Chaletpools; V S Pritchett and Chatto & Windus for an abridged extract from *Midnight Oil*; Resort Services Department, Brighton Borough Council for an extract from their tourist guide; Laurie Lee and Andre Deutsch for an extract from *I Can't Stay Long* (1975); Bernard Schofield and Cassell Co. Ltd., a division of Macmillan Publishing Co. for an extract from *The Urban Dweller's Country Almanac*; SM Publications Limited for an extract from *Slimming Magazine's Your Greatest Guide to Calories*; Save the Children for an extract from one of their fund-raising leaflets; Anthony Carson, Collins Publishers and Punch for an extract from *A Book of Railway Journeys* by Ludovic Kennedy; London Borough of Camden for material from their leaflet on equal opportunities; Northern and Shell Limited for extracts from the Ioniser article in *Next* (January 1983); John Brookes and Marshall Cavendish Books Limited for two extracts from *The Small Garden*; Colin Riach and Radio Times for material from a 'Medical Express' article; Jonathan Raban and Collins Publishers for an abridged extract from *Arabia Through the Looking Glass*.

Copyright photographs are reproduced by courtesy of the following:

Network p.17; Farmer's Weekly p.37; Sally and Richard Greenhill p.57; Barnaby's p.94; VRU p.75.

Contents

Notes to the Student

Test One

Paper 1	1
Paper 2	7
Paper 3	8
Paper 4	13
Paper 5	17

Test Two

Paper 1	20
Paper 2	26
Paper 3	27
Paper 4	32
Paper 5	37

Test Three

Paper 1	40
Paper 2	46
Paper 3	47
Paper 4	52
Paper 5	57

Test Four

Paper 1	59
Paper 2	65
Paper 3	66
Paper 4	71
Paper 5	75

Test Five

Paper 1	77
Paper 2	84
Paper 3	85
Paper 4	90
Paper 5	94

Appendix: Prescribed Texts   97

Notes to the Student

The object of this book is to provide students preparing for the Cambridge Certificate of Proficiency in English with complete practice in the Written and Oral papers. Each of the five tests consists of three written and two oral papers as follows:

WRITTEN PAPERS

Paper 1 Reading Comprehension (1 hour)

Section A Twenty-five multiple choice questions testing vocabulary and formal grammatical control, in sentence contexts.

Section B Fifteen multiple choice reading comprehension questions based on three or more texts, designed to test gist, detailed content, implied meaning, etc. In one passage recognition of form, register and intention will be required. Texts may include information in graphic form.

Paper 2 Composition (2 hours)

Two compositions from a choice of descriptive, situational or discursive topics, or topics based on prescribed reading. Assessment will be based on organisation and clarity of content, accuracy of grammatical control, fluency and range of expression.

Paper 3 Use of English (2 hours)

Section A Open-completion or transformation items designed to test active control of the patterns and usage of English.

Section B Questions on a passage designed to test ability to understand, interpret and summarise.

ORAL PAPERS

Paper 4 Listening Comprehension (Approx. 30 minutes)

Questions of varying type (selection, re-ordering, blank-filling etc.) to test accurate understanding of spoken English, based on recorded material including conversation, announcements etc.

Paper 5 Interview (Approx. 20 minutes)

(i) Conversation on a picture stimulus, assessed on fluency and grammatical accuracy.

(ii) Reading aloud of a short passage (announcement, instruction or situation), assessed on pronunciation of individual sounds and on stress and linking in phrases.

(iii) Structured communication exercise (role-play, discussion etc, on prescribed texts or unprepared material), assessed on communicative ability and vocabulary.

A Teacher's Edition of this Book is available, with Answer Key and Tapescript.

A set of 3 examination format cassettes of the Listening Comprehension material for Paper 4 is available. The passages for reading aloud from Paper 5 are also included.

Test One

PAPER 1   READING COMPREHENSION   (1 hour)

SECTION A

In this section you must choose the word or phrase which best completes each sentence. Indicate the letter A, B, C or D against the number of each item 1 to 25 for the word or phrase you choose. **Give one answer only** *to each question.*

1   Charity for the Aged is mainly staffed by .... workers.
    A free   B voluntary   C willing   D unsolicited

2   He is a .... supporter of nuclear disarmament.
    A resolved   B persevering   C staunch   D unbeaten

3   The proposal to build a new town hall was .... by the council.
    A thrown away   B thrown in   C thrown out   D thrown off

4   Please close the window; there's a terrible ....
    A current   B breeze   C headwind   D draught

5   The parliamentary candidate was .... by several people at the meeting.
    A heckled   B banned   C dissented   D objected

6   There has been an encouraging .... to the appeal for donations to the Famine Relief Fund.
    A reply   B response   C return   D acknowledgement

7   Aluminium is the most plentiful metal in the Earth's ....
    A surface   B crust   C exterior   D cap

8   I can't see anybody today; I'm .... in work.
    A round my neck   B over the top   C up to my eyes   D round the bend

9   Since he saw that programme on television, he has become .... with physical fitness.
    A concentrated   B obsessed   C engrossed   D penetrated

10 The ambassador presented his .... to the Queen.
    A credentials   B references   C documentations   D depositions

11 Barry Masters has been .... as a candidate for the Surrey by-election.
    A named   B called   C announced   D nominated

12 It's very strange but I had .... that the plane would crash.
    A an omen   B a prediction   C a presentiment   D an intuition

1

13 The clerk was dismissed for being .... in his duties.
    A negligent   B forgetful   C unmindful   D indifferent

14 The dispute between the unions and management will have to be settled
    by ....
    A judgement   B arbitration   C verdict   D adjudication

15 At first sight the island seemed to be bare and .... of any kind of vegetation.
    A vacant   B absent   C devoid   D minus

16 Most of the poet's earlier work was published under a ....
    A namesake   B misnomer   C nickname   D pseudonym

17 Although their advertising methods are rather ...., they seem to produce
    results.
    A unconventional   B uncomfortable   C unaccustomed   D unexampled

18 Although he hasn't got any academic qualifications, he has a lot of practical
    experience ....
    A in his grasp   B at his fingertips   C under his belt   D at his back

19 Nobody likes him because he is always trying to .... favour with the boss.
    A ingratiate   B curry   C obtain   D cook

20 In a multi-racial society, it is important to preserve the .... culture of its
    members.
    A tribal   B biological   C national   D ethnic

21 The suspect is .... to have been in the neighbourhood at the time of the
    crime.
    A affirmed   B alleged   C accused   D announced

22 I must have .... for ten minutes before the telephone operator put me
    through.
    A hung about   B hung up   C hung on   D hung round

23 As you can see, this is a highly .... computer system.
    A sophisticated   B intelligent   C composite   D harmonised

24 After he had lived in Britain for six years, he applied for ....
    A residency   B nationality   C naturalisation   D commonalty

25 We .... the boat by the bank.
    A fastened   B tied   C docked   D moored

2

*In this section you will find after each of the passages a number of questions or unfinished statements about the passage, each with four suggested answers or ways of finishing. You must choose the one which you think fits best. Underline the letter A, B, C or D against the number of each item, 26 to 40, for the answer you choose. **Give one answer only** to each question. Read each passage right through before choosing your answers.*

FIRST PASSAGE

There is not much to say about most aeroplane journeys. Anything remarkable must be disastrous, so you define a good flight by negatives; you didn't get hijacked, you didn't crash, you didn't throw up, you weren't late, you weren't nauseated by the food. So you are grateful. The gratitude brings such relief your mind goes blank, which is appropriate, for the aeroplane passenger is a time-traveller. He crawls into a carpeted tube that is reeking of disinfectant; he is strapped in to go home, or away. Time is truncated, or in any case warped; he leaves in one time-zone and emerges in another. And from the moment he steps into the tube and braces his knees on the seat in front, uncomfortably upright—from the moment he departs, his mind is focused on arrival. That is, if he has any sense at all. If he looked out of the window he would see nothing but the tundra of the cloud layer, and above is empty space. Time is brilliantly blinded: there is nothing to see. This is the reason why so many people are apologetic about taking planes. They say, 'What I'd really like to do is forget these plastic jumbos and get a three-masted schooner and just stand there on the poop deck with the wind in my hair.'

But apologies are not necessary. An aeroplane flight may not be travel in any accepted sense, but it certainly is magic. Anyone with the price of a ticket can conjure up the castled crag of Drachenfels or the Lake Isle of Innisfree by simply using the right escalator at, say, Logan Airport in Boston—but it must be said that there is probably more to animate the mind, more of travel, in that one ascent on the escalator, than in the whole plane journey put together.

26 According to the writer, an uneventful flight
   A increases your self-confidence.
   B negates your personality.
   C has no positive effect.
   D produces amnesia.

27 The writer describes an aeroplane passenger as a 'time-traveller' because he
   A loses his sense of time.
   B is suspended in time.
   C attaches no importance to time.
   D has to adjust to time changes.

28 Why do people often apologise for travelling by plane? They
   A have nothing else to say.
   B don't want to seem unadventurous.
   C are afraid of boring their listeners.
   D don't want to appear boastful.

29 In the writer's opinion the magic of travelling by air is its power to
   A stimulate our imagination.
   B indulge our whims.
   C flatter our intelligence.
   D broaden our minds.

WATER EMERGENCY

ADVICE FROM THE INSTITUTE OF ENVIRONMENTAL HEALTH OFFICERS

The water supply may be of low pressure, discoloured, intermittent or fail completely due to industrial dispute and the dispute may also prevent the provision of adequate emergency supplies or repairing of bursts.

During the current dispute, all householders and people involved in any food preparation are advised to take the following steps:-

All water used for drinking, food preparation, including ice making, and cleaning teeth should be boiled briskly for at least 1 minute. Sterilising tablets should not be regarded as an adequate substitute for boiling.

Keep a reasonable amount of boiled water in a clean covered container in case your supply fails without warning, but if not used within 24 hours discard and boil a fresh supply.

All cooking utensils, crockery and cutlery should be washed in boiled water.

Water, unless previously boiled, should not be added to washing-up water. Boiling water for washing-up should, preferably, be allowed to cool to hand-hot temperature.

Do not rinse utensils, crockery and glasses under the cold water tap.

A suitable detergent/steriliser should be added to washing-up water in the quantities quoted on the product. Detergents alone do not make the water safe.

If dishwashing machines are used, the detergent/steriliser recommended by the manufacturer should be used.

If no detergent/steriliser is available, (and remember normal washing-up liquid is not a sterilant) add the normal washing-up liquid together with a weak solution of bleach in the quantity of 5 ml per litre of boiled water.

Food preparation surfaces should be wiped over with a preferably disposable, cloth soaked in a weak solution of bleach (ie. 5 ml per litre of water).

Even though water may be discoloured it can still be used after boiling. The quality can be improved if it is strained through a handkerchief or muslin before boiling (any straining cloth to be boiled before re-use) and this may be especially applicable for babies in the preparation of a feed or sterilising bottles and teats, (eg. making up solutions of a hypochlorite - a steriliser). Babies' feeds should be only made with boiled water.

Do not wash vehicles or use water wastefully. If the mains supply is cut off flushing toilets will be difficult but any water available should be used for this purpose.

Water must be boiled before incorporation into ice lollies or similar products, or dehydrated food.

G. Taylor

District Medical Officer   27 January 1983

30 This warning has been given owing to
    A   the contamination of main water supplies.
    B   urgent repair of burst water mains.
    C   industrial action by public employees.
    D   total failure in water supplies.

31 It has been circulated in the form of
    A   a broadcast announcement.
    B   a circular distributed to the public.
    C   a newspaper article.
    D   an advertisement in a magazine.

32 When preparing meals, people are advised to
    A   sterilise all food.
    B   keep all food covered.
    C   discard all unused water.
    D   use previously boiled water.

33 As a safety measure, the public are warned not to
    A   rely on the use of detergents.
    B   rinse crockery in hand-hot water.
    C   use detergents for washing-up.
    D   use a dishwashing machine.

34 To conserve water supplies, discoloured water
    A   should not be given to babies.
    B   improves if strained after boiling.
    C   may be filtered before boiling.
    D   is unsuitable for drinking purposes.

THIRD PASSAGE

Extract 1

Although the heyday of the balloon and airship has long since passed, they are still occasionally to be seen in the skies. Ballooning has become a popular minority sport, and international balloon meetings are held at various centres each year. Hot-air, hydrogen and helium balloons all have their devotees.

The overall design of balloons has changed little over the years. They have a spherical or pear-shaped bag, or envelope, made of gas-tight material. This is now generally a coated polyester plastic like Mylar or Dacron. From the envelope is suspended a basket which carries the crew.

The principle upon which balloon flight depends was first stated by the Greek scientist Archimedes. Any object will float in a fluid (liquid or gas) if it displaces a weight of fluid equal to its own weight. If it displaces a weight of fluid greater than its own weight, it will experience an upthrust which will carry it upwards. So you need to fill a balloon with the lightest possible gas for maximum uplift.

Extract 2

In recent years renewed interest has been shown in airships, and people in the know are forecasting that they could once more become commercially successful, operating as both passenger and freight carriers. With the costs of conventional airline travel ever-rising, airships should be able to offer a competitive service. And, although they would fly much slower than aeroplanes, they would save time by operating directly from sites in city centres.

Typical of these airships is the Goodyear 'Europa', one of a fleet of six. The cigar-shaped envelope, which is made of double-ply coated Dacron, measures 58 m and has a maximum diameter of 14 m. The small cabin, or gondola, beneath the envelope can carry a pilot and up to six passengers. Mounted behind it are two six-cylinder petrol engines. Less conventional designs have been suggested for the airships of the future. One is shaped like a saucer, a design which appears to be more stable in flight than the traditional cigar-shape.

Extract 3

Whether 'flying-saucer' airships take to the skies or not, aviation will be dominated by the aeroplane for the foreseeable future. Whereas an airship obtains its lift statically by means of lighter-than-air gases, a plane obtains its lift aerodynamically, that is, by moving through the air. When any object moves through the air, it interacts with the air and experiences forces that cause it to move this way and that. This will be familiar to anyone who has put his hand out of the window of a moving car.

By inclining your hand upwards slightly into the airstream, you notice that the aerodynamic forces cause it to rise. Herein lies the key to aeroplane flight. To make a plane fly you must attach to it surfaces which are inclined slightly into the airstream so that they experience a net upward force, or lift. The surfaces that generate the lift in a plane are the wings.

35 The crew of a balloon
   A are suspended from a basket.
   B float in a plastic envelope.
   C travel beneath the envelope.
   D travel in a pear-shaped bag.

36 What causes a balloon to be carried upwards?
   A It is heavier than air.
   B It is lighter than the air it displaces.
   C It displaces air equal to its own weight.
   D It is filled with gas.

37 Experts say that airships may offer a competitive form of air travel because they
   A can come and go in urban areas.
   B can carry passengers and freight.
   C are safer because they fly slowly.
   D are not subject to flight regulations.

38 In extracts 1 and 2 what similarities are given between an airship and a balloon?
   A Purpose of flight.
   B Type of gas used.
   C Passenger/crew accommodation.
   D Design of envelope.

39 What, according to extract 3, causes an aeroplane to lift?
   A Being lighter than air.
   B Being lighter than gas.
   C Remaining static in an airstream.
   D Interaction with the air.

40 Compared with airships, travel by plane
   A is unlikely to become obsolete.
   B is likely to be cheaper and faster.
   C will become less popular.
   D will be unaffected by competition.

PAPER 2 COMPOSITION (2 hours)

*Write **two only** of the following composition exercises. Your answers must follow exactly the instructions given.*

1   Write a descriptive account of any sporting event you have attended. (About 350 words)

2   Write a balanced discussion on the theme 'The role of the artist in society'. You may write in the form of a dialogue between two speakers, or in essay form. (About 350 words)

3   Describe the major tourist attractions in your country. (About 200 words)

4   A nuclear power station is to be built in your area. This will involve the demolition of homes, schools and pasture. Write a letter of protest to your local newspaper setting forth your views why the power station should be sited elsewhere. (About 200 words)

5   (See Appendix: Prescribed texts)

PAPER 3   USE OF ENGLISH   (2 hours)

SECTION A

1   *Fill each of the numbered blanks in the following passage with* **one** *suitable word.*

Customs officers at London Airport yesterday .... (1) £50,000 .... (2) of illegal drugs which were being smuggled into Britain in .... (3) labelled 'Urgent Medical Supplies'. The authorities have suspected for .... (4) time that drugs were being brought into the country in this .... (5). The operation is believed to be the work of a .... (6) organised international gang. Four men were arrested at the airport and .... (7) for questioning, but it is unlikely that they are the .... (8). In fact they declared that they were .... (9) of what the boxes contained and had acted in good .... (10) in bringing them into Britain. This is the third time .... (11) six months that .... (12) have been made to smuggle illegal goods .... (13) Customs by declaring them to be medical supplies. They are frequently .... (14) in airtight containers and a warning is given that they may deteriorate if they are tampered .... (15). 'We are .... (16) to put a stop to this practice,' said one of the customs officers today. 'There is .... (17) way these people are going to get away with this .... (18) longer. We have the .... (19) co-operation of Interpol who are as anxious as we are to track .... (20) the main source of supply.'

8

2 *Finish each of the following sentences in such a way that it means exactly the same as the sentence printed before it.*

      EXAMPLE: 'I'm sorry to have kept you waiting,' he said to me.

      ANSWER: He apologised *for keeping me waiting.*

  a) The manager said the work must be finished by 6 p.m.
      The manager insisted on ....

  b) There are no seats available for tonight's performance.
      Tonight's performance is ....

  c) He was driving so fast that he was stopped by the police.
      The police ....

  d) Passengers must not cross the lines at any time.
      It is ....

  e) Fortunately, there were no casualties as a result of the air crash.
      Fortunately, no one ....

  f) The terrorists threatened to kill the hostages if their demands were not met.
      The terrorists declared their ....

  g) I was not convinced by his argument.
      I didn't ....

  h) Your season ticket is only valid till 31 December.
      You can't use ....

3 *Fill each of the numbered blanks with a suitable word or phrase.*

      EXAMPLE: The plane was delayed for five hours *owing to bad* weather.

  a) She was sent to hospital for .... knee.

  b) Do hurry up or .... our flight.

  c) He never thinks of .... himself.

  d) If you think you've got flu, you'd .... to bed.

  e) The twins are so alike, I .... the other.

  f) I don't remember .... beautiful sunset before.

4　For each of the sentences below, write a new sentence as similar as possible in meaning to the original sentence, but using the words given: these words must **not be altered** in any way.

　　　　EXAMPLE: Is it really necessary for you to play your radio so loudly?
　　　　　　　　have

　　　　ANSWER: *Do you have to play your radio so loudly?*

a)　There is a great deal of poverty in that area.
　　poor

　　..

b)　We must make sure this doesn't happen again.
　　steps

　　..

c)　I think you've got your sweater on back to front.
　　wrong

　　..

d)　The driver died as a result of the accident.
　　fatally

　　..

e)　I don't approve of the way he treats his staff.
　　attitude

　　..

f)　Considering he's deaf, I think he did very well in the oral exam.
　　taking

　　..

g)　It's a difficult problem, but I'm sure it's not insurmountable.
　　solve

　　..

h)　I don't agree with his views on nuclear disarmament.
　　differ

　　..

SECTION B

5 *Read the following passage, then answer the questions which follow it.*

By about 70,000 B.C. man had made further progress in overcoming his environment. He lived in caves and knew how to make fire. He kept himself warm by wearing skin clothing. The dominant species at the time was Neanderthal man, of whom many fossils survive. His stone tools were made from thick flakes of stone, finished by fine
5 chipping. In their burial of the dead, the Neanderthals showed a great cultural advance.

The short, thickset and beetle-browed Neanderthals were ousted from the evolutionary scene by the direct ancestors of modern man, a breed we call the Cromagnons. Tall and well built, the Cromagnons had a long skull, narrow nose and
10 prominent chin. Their brain capacity was, if anything, greater than our own. Their stone tools were the most sophisticated yet. They struck thin, narrow blades from a prepared core and fashioned them into numerous tools, such as knives, scrapers and awls. More important was their manufacture of specialist tools, or burins—sharp-edged chisels and gravers—for working antler, bone and ivory. It has been said that
15 these burins were the forerunners of machine tools—tools made to shape other implements.

With greater guile than their forebears, the Cromagnons found hunting easy on the steppe and tundra, which teemed with bison, reindeer and mammoth. This allowed them more leisure, which they soon put to good use. They radically improved their
20 weaponry, adding flint tips to their spears and making spear throwers to launch them with greater force. They invented the bow and arrow, which revolutionised hunting, for it enabled the hunter to kill his prey from a safer distance.

These early men extended their mastery over their environment when they learned how to make lamps. These lamps were hollowed-out stones or shells filled with animal
25 oil or fat, into which dipped a crude form of wick. When you consider how important artificial light is to us today, the invention of the lamp can be seen in true perspective.

Increased leisure also allowed the advanced hunters ample time for artistic pursuits. They became skilful carvers, competent sculptors and consummate painters. The breathtakingly beautiful cave paintings of Lascaux in France and Altamira in Spain
30 represent the summit of their achievement.

a) What was the most significant advance in the development of Neanderthal man?

....

b) Explain the meaning of 'flakes' (line 4).

....

c) How did early man make tools?

....

d) Give another word or phrase for 'ousted' (line 7).

....

e) In what way did the physical appearance of the Cromagnons differ from the Neanderthals?

....

f) What does the phrase 'if anything' (line 10) mean?

....

g) Why are their stone tools described as the 'most sophisticated' (line 11)?

....

h) Where did the Cromagnons find good hunting grounds?

....

i) To what does 'this' in line 18 refer?

....

j) What was the effect of the invention of the bow and arrow?

....

k) How did the Cromagnons create artificial light?

....

l) How else did the Cromagnons employ their leisure time?

....

m) Give another word or phrase for 'consummate' (line 28).

....

n) Give two surviving examples of their artistic achievement.

....

o) Summarise in 50 to 100 words the progress made by the Cromagnons.

....

....

....

....

....

....

PAPER 4 LISTENING COMPREHENSION (Approx. 30 minutes)

FIRST PART

For each of the questions 1—5 put a tick ($\checkmark$) in one of the boxes, A, B, C or D.

1 The Bailiwick of Guernsey is

   A the capital of the Channel Islands.

   B part of Northern France.

   C a United Kingdom dominion.

   D a British possession.

A	
B	
C	
D	

2 The British connection with Guernsey dates from

   A the coronation of William II.

   B the latter half of the 11th century.

   C the invasion of France in 1066.

   D the Norman invasion in the 10th century.

A	
B	
C	
D	

3 Under the feudal system the landowners

   A fought to protect their workers.

   B allowed their workers special privileges.

   C assumed responsibility for their workers.

   D did not recognise any rights but their own.

A	
B	
C	
D	

4 The Government of Guernsey is

   A administered from Whitehall.

   B unchanged after 900 years.

   C not accountable to the British Government.

   D subject to British jurisdiction.

A	
B	
C	
D	

5 The role of the Lieutenant Governor appointed by the Queen is to

   A represent the British Home Office.

   B act as Head of State.

   C ratify laws passed by 'The States'.

   D liaise between Great Britain and Guernsey.

A	
B	
C	
D	

6   The unique feature of 'The States' is that it has

    A   a non-political administration.

    B   an all-party government.

    C   a one-party administration.

    D   equal representation.

A	
B	
C	
D	

SECOND PART

For questions 1 and 2 look at the lists of objects and actions. For each of the questions 3—6 put a tick in one of the boxes A, B, C or D.

1   In addition to a speaker, which of these things do you need to make a battery from a lemon?
    Tick the boxes where appropriate.

A	Fuse wire	
B	Scissors	
C	Copper Coin	
D	Metal Plate	

E	Knife	
F	Cooking foil	
G	Light bulb	
H	Paper clips	

2   To make the battery, in what order would you do these things? Write the letter in the appropriate box.

A	Connect coin and foil with fuse wire.
B	Make two slits in the lemon.
C	Connect coin and foil to the speaker.
D	Put coin and foil in the slits.

1	
2	
3	
4	

3   At first Harry thinks that John is

    A   making fun of him.

    B   having him on.

    C   trying to impress him.

    D   humouring him.

A	
B	
C	
D	

4   An electrolyte is

    A   a lamp bulb.

    B   a lightning conductor.

    C   an electric current.

    D   a power conductor.

A	
B	
C	
D	

5 If you touch the connected fuse wire with your tongue you can test if it

    A has come alive.

    B is electrically charged.

    C makes a crackling sound.

    D is battery-powered.

A	
B	
C	
D	

6 In spite of what John tells him Harry seems

    A incredulous.

    B amused.

    C unenthusiastic.

    D confused.

A	
B	
C	
D	

THIRD PART

For each of the questions 1—4 put a tick (✓) in one of the boxes, A, B, C or D.

1 Margery Hooper is speaking to students

    A at a music conference.

    B on a holiday course.

    C at a holiday resort.

    D on a training course.

A	
B	
C	
D	

2 The guitar course

    A will not be held at Grange Manor.

    B will involve some travelling.

    C is an innovation at Grange Manor.

    D will last less than three weeks.

A	
B	
C	
D	

3 Students requiring course materials should

    A buy them from the secretary.

    B buy them in the main hall.

    C register with the secretary.

    D go to the bookshop after 10 a.m.

A	
B	
C	
D	

4 Students wishing to go on excursions are requested to

A book in good time.

B produce their course number.

C book the coach direct.

D note the coach number.

A	
B	
C	
D	

FOURTH PART

For questions 1 and 2 look at the International Music Programme, and for question 3 look at the list of categories of people.

International Music Programme

20th to 27th May

Day	Date	Type of Music	Reduced prices
Sunday	20		Senior Citizen
Monday	21		Children
Tuesday	22		Students
Wednesday	23	English	Family Groups
Thursday	24		Disabled
Friday	25		Unemployed
Saturday	26	Indian	
Sunday	27		

1 Which type of music can you hear on two evenings in the week?

....

2 Fill in the spaces on the music programme above.

3 Look at the categories of people in the list. Tick the box beside those people who are eligible for reduced price tickets.

16

PAPER 5 INTERVIEW (Approx. 20 minutes)

(i) *Look at this picture carefully and be prepared to answer some questions about it.*

1   What is different about the people in this picture?

2   Where might it be?

3   Describe the couple on the right.

4   What do you think the man on the left is thinking?

Rich v. poor
Importance of clothes
People's image

(ii)   *Look at this passage and be prepared to answer some questions about it and then to read it aloud.*

AN ARGUMENT FOR HEALTHY LIVING
THAT HOLDS WATER BEAUTIFULLY!

Who said you can't buy health and happiness? With a Pinelog chaletpool you can enjoy the prospect of exhilarating relaxation, soothe away muscular aches and pains, celebrate a return to glowing good health—and have some good, family fun into the bargain.

Wallow in hydrotherapeutic splendour as powerful jets, at a temperature of 90 °F, lull you into a state of luxurious well-being. And without going to great lengths, practise your long distance swimming on the spot, against the powerful swim jet at the opposite end of the pool.

SAMPLE QUESTIONS

What do you think this comes from?
What are you being asked to invest in?
How would it benefit you?

Now read the passage aloud.

(iii)   *There may be a variety of options offered in this section. Choose one of the following:*

a)   Discussion.

Be prepared to discuss a subject initiated by the examiner, for example:
Technology

You may be invited to give your comments on various aspects, such as:
effects on society
changing work patterns
automation

If you are participating in a group discussion you might be asked to speak individually about one of these categories.

b)

A	B
You arranged to meet your friend outside the cinema at 7.00. It is now 7.45 and your friend has just arrived. You speak first.	You arranged to meet your friend outside the cinema at 8.00. You arrive early at 7.45 but your friend is already there. He/she speaks to you first.

(Two candidates or candidate/examiner hold conversation.)

c)   Prescribed texts—See Appendix.

PAPER 1 READING COMPREHENSION (1 hour)

SECTION A

In this section you must choose the word or phrase which best completes each sentence.
Indicate the letter A, B, C or D against the number of each item 1 to 25 for the word or
phrase you choose. **Give one answer only** *to each question.*

1 This is an exciting book which .... new ground in educational research.
   A scratches   B breaks   C reaches   D turns

2 .... you find yourself in difficulty, please ask for help.
   A Could   B May   C Should   D Might

3 Overweight people have .... to avoid exercise.
   A an inclination   B a tendency   C a disposition   D an affectation

4 The second .... of cakes turned out much better than the first.
   A batch   B set   C group   D bunch

5 Always use a suntan cream to protect your skin against the harmful effect of the
   sun's ....
   A beams   B rays   C light   D waves

6 He felt he would never .... the shock of being made redundant.
   A get through   B get by   C get over   D get off

7 It is .... that nuclear power stations can produce cheap electricity.
   A proclaimed   B commented   C warranted   D claimed

8 The police car raced down the street with the .... blaring.
   A siren   B gong   C bell   D alarm

9 Some language students reach a high .... of competence in communication.
   A level   B note   C grade   D mark

10 Wearing a car seat belt is considered by some people as an unnecessary .... of
   the freedom of the individual.
   A constriction   B restriction   C compression   D repression

11 It is sometimes difficult to know if somebody is .... or telling the truth.
   A deluding   B intriguing   C bluffing   D mystifying

12 As the weather became colder, the rain .... sleet.
   A came to   B went to   C passed to   D turned to

13 He had not realised the extent to which such fear was .... in himself.
   A tacit   B covert   C latent   D inert

14 The workers tried to .... the experience to their own lives.
   A accord   B credit   C refer   D relate

15 The room was in a terrible mess with a .... of clothes all over the floor.
   A jumble   B mixture   C litter   D huddle

16 One of the multinationals is expected to make a take-over .... for the engineering company.
   A bet   B bid   C offer   D bribe

17 He always considered the history degree as a .... in his life.
   A tide-mark   B millstone   C landmark   D signpost

18 .... a week goes by without some educational problem arising.
   A Infrequently   B Hardly   C Practically   D Merely

19 The children's TV programmes were so successful that a .... series is being made.
   A by-product   B backup   C follow-up   D after-effect

20 The shop assistant .... her shoulders indifferently.
   A twitched   B flexed   C raised   D shrugged

21 If you do not have ready cash, you can always buy the goods on .... purchase.
   A rent   B hire   C land   D borrow

22 You cannot ignore the situation forever, one day you will have to .... the consequences of your act.
   A look up to   B wake up to   C stand up to   D face up to

23 Unsuitable recruits should be .... before they start training.
   A weeded out   B narrowed down   C laid aside   D passed over

24 She was very enthusiastic about sailing around the world and now was just .... to go.
   A leaping   B raring   C bounding   D jumping

25 The devaluation should .... better chances for exports.
   A bring out   B set up   C account for   D lead to

*In this section you will find after each of the passages a number of questions or unfinished statements about the passage, each with four suggested answers or ways of finishing. You must choose the one you think fits best. Underline the letter A, B, C or D against the number of each item, 26 to 40, for the answer you choose. **Give one answer only** to each question. Read each passage right through before choosing your answers.*

FIRST PASSAGE

For a very long time dowsing has been looked upon by many people with scepticism and suspicion, or simply designated under the label of the supernatural which defies logical explanation. Both these viewpoints do little justice to what is now becoming appreciated as a skill, although a paranormal skill, but one which is not beyond the man in the street. Indeed the art of dowsing has undergone a considerable revival of interest of late. But can anyone really dowse? Well, it is said that no one can teach you, the most anyone can do is help you to learn. It would appear that an awareness and feel for the medium is very important, but as with any other skill, practice is the governing factor.

What exactly is dowsing? Many of us will associate it with the image of a man holding a forked hazel twig in his hands, walking across a field in search of subterranean water which will manifest its presence by forcing the end of the stick downwards to the ground. While this image is by no means inaccurate, it is nevertheless a popular myth which has obliterated the true nature of dowsing with its far wider implications. In simple terms, dowsing is a method of using an implement to find hidden material by a non-physical means. The dowser concentrates his mind on the subject of his search while the implement in his hands focuses the unconscious awareness of the dowser's perception of that subject. Although searching for underground water supplies is the most popular application of dowsing, it is also widely used for discovering mineral deposits such as coal, iron and precious metals. It is also used to find lost objects, or dead bodies in police investigations, to determine the position of archaeological remains, and to find missing relatives. In fact there is no end to the practical uses to which dowsing can be applied.

The forked hazel stick is another popular myth because not only will any forked stick serve as a dowsing instrument but also bent metal rods or wires, or even one long rod with a right-angle bend to hold. There are a number of plausible explanations of how it works and many dowsers have their own ideas as to what causes their particular reaction and response to the presence of the material being searched for. Some say it is unconscious neuro-muscular contractions which affect the stick or rod, while another explanation claims the dowser actually 'tunes in' to the material through his paranormal awareness of its presence. Some dowsers claim they are even able to see the underground material of their search. Yet others say it is an instinct, the same as that used by some animals who live in the desert to discern water under the sand. A recent explanation is that all substances give off radiations which the dowser with his paranormal perception picks up through the medium of his stick or rod. As of yet there is no concrete or scientific explanation as to how dowsing really works, but no doubt, in time, scientists will be able to rationalise what actually happens and enlighten us all.

26 The writer thinks it is possible for anyone to become a dowser because
   A it doesn't need paranormal skill.
   B no logical understanding is needed.
   C very little practice is necessary.
   D no particular sensitivity is required.

27 A popular myth about dowsing is
   A not everyone can do it.
   B it can only be done in fields.
   C it only works for men, not women.
   D only one type of implement can be used.

28 As well as indicating the source of underground water, dowsing is also used for
   A discovering antiques.
   B uncovering buried corpses.
   C locating ancient ruins.
   D finding precious stones.

29 Most people think that a dowsing tool is
   A shaped like the letter Y.
   B bent into a letter T.
   C formed like the letter L.
   D joined to form a V.

30 One explanation given by the dowsers to explain their powers is that they
   A have X-ray eyesight.
   B are radioactive.
   C have extrasensory perception.
   D have well-developed muscles.

SECOND PASSAGE

In 1963 an American physiotherapist Glenn Doman wrote a best-selling book called *How to Teach Your Baby to Read*. Now translated into 17 languages, this book arose from his work with brain-damaged children in Pennsylvania. Doman and his team of specialists had wondered why brain-injured children didn't improve with treatment. Then they realised that orthodox methods of treatment only relieved the symptoms, not the problem, which of course was the brain itself. So they developed a new approach.

'All we do for all children here is to give them visual, auditory and tactile stimulation with increased frequency, intensity and duration, in recognition of the orderly way in which the brain grows,' says Doman. 'The result was that by 1960 we had hundreds of severely brain-injured two-year-olds who could read and understand.' The team had discovered that even children who had half their brains removed could, by stimulation, achieve higher IQs than the average normal child.

Then the team began to think if such amazing results could be achieved with brain-damaged children, what would happen if the same treatment were given to normal children. So eight years ago the Better Baby Institute was opened for the benefit of normal children. The same stimulating enriched environment was provided, and, by the time the children left, around seven years old, they could generally speak and read three foreign languages, play a musical instrument, read three full-length books a week *and* do all the other things that a so-called 'normal' child could do.

In Doman's view, the child's passion to learn during the years up to six, must be fed. He believes that, like muscles, the brain develops with use, especially so in those first few years.

Nowadays, parents come from all over the world to Pennsylvania to see and learn from the work of Doman and his team; they want to discover how they can fulfil their roles as nature's teachers, by using their love, understanding and instincts for the benefit of their children. For in the words of Doman, 'Every child born has a greater potential intelligence than Leonardo da Vinci used'.

31 In his research, Glenn Doman discovered that brain-damaged children improved when they
    A   were taught to read and understand.
    B   could speak several languages.
    C   got the right treatment.
    D   got relief for their symptoms.

32 Doman's new approach was to
    A   increase the number of types of stimulation.
    B   give shorter periods of decreased stimulation.
    C   intensify the shorter periods of stimulation.
    D   decrease the time between the periods of stimulation.

33 From information in the text, we can assume that
    A   most normal two-year-old children can read.
    B   brain-damaged children can overcome their disability.
    C   brain-damaged children generally have high IQs.
    D   children with only half a brain are more intelligent.

34 At the Better Baby Institute
    A   the idea of 'normal' achievement was challenged.
    B   children needed seven years to develop normality.
    C   unnatural development of children was achieved.
    D   children developed at a normal standard rate.

35 Parents come to the Institute because they want
    A   their children to become as intelligent as Leonardo da Vinci.
    B   to learn how to teach their children about nature.
    C   to develop their own abilities to help their children.
    D   their children to develop instincts of love and understanding.

THIRD PASSAGE

Extract 1

A computer is an 'information processor'. It is given information, called 'data', instructed to do certain things to it and then show us the results. The data put into the computer is called the 'input' and the results which come out are the 'output'. Some people say the circle of large standing stones at Stonehenge is a kind of computer. Prehistoric people worked out their calendar from the position of the shadows made by the sun shining on the stones. If you think of the stones as a computer, the sunlight is the input and the calendar is the output.

Extract 2

Teach yourself new subjects and skills at your own pace with a home computer. Use it to help with schoolwork, for self-improvement, even to improve your career skills. Learn touch-typing, foreign languages or computer programming. Compose music, arrange harmony or play your favourite tunes. A home computer can help children of all ages learn classroom subjects such as spelling, geography and others. In fact it makes learning fun. So if you want to teach yourself, or help your children teach themselves—get a home computer. It can also help you manage your personal finances; help you to work out taxes and plan household budgets, or keep track of financial transactions. You can make business a pleasure with a home computer.

Extract 3

If you have a computer, or are about to buy one, sooner or later you're bound to come up against the problem of what to do with it. After all you have at your fingertips a device that can be told what to do—the only problem is how. For in order to run a ready-made program it is not enough to just insert the tape or disk in the appropriate place and turn on the machine. The computer needs to be told to find out what's on the tape or disk and then told to start doing whatever the tape or disk tells it to do. These operations are usually called 'loading' and 'running', and to tell the computer to perform them, you usually need to type something on the keyboard—generally the words 'load' and 'run'. Now if you can load and run a ready-made program, you have already mastered the essentials of computer programming.

36 Why is the use of words such as 'input' and 'output' in extract 1 important?
    A   It introduces people to computer language.
    B   It shows computer language is the same as English.
    C   It helps people understand an unknown language.
    D   It gives people access to a scientific language.

37 What is the purpose of talking about Stonehenge in extract 1?
    A   To give an example of the very first computer.
    B   To provide a means of relating the past and present.
    C   To present an alternative way of explaining computers.
    D   To show that computers are older than mankind.

38 Extract 2 is probably taken from
    A a manufacturer's brochure.
    B an educational leaflet.
    C a teach-yourself computer book.
    D a children's guide to computers.

39 Extracts 1 and 3 deal with
    A information about computer programs.
    B the historical background to computers.
    C do-it-yourself computer instruction.
    D a general introduction to computers.

40 Compared with extract 3, the usefulness of a computer as described in extract 2
    appears to
    A depend on extensive utilisation.
    B rely on complicated programming.
    C involve the use of children.
    D depend on the type of computer.

PAPER 2 COMPOSITION (2 hours)

*Write **two only** of the following composition exercises. Your answers must follow exactly the instructions given.*

1 Write a descriptive account of a journey made in bad weather. (About 350 words)

2 Write a balanced discussion on the theme 'Freedom is an Illusion'. You may write in the form of a dialogue between two speakers, or in essay form. (About 350 words)

3 Describe the importance and influence of a recent event in your country. (About 200 words)

4 You have just listened to the following message on your answerphone. Write the main points and make notes of the talk you have been asked to give. (About 200 words)

Hi, this is Andrea at the Students' Union. Uhh, do you think you could come along and speak to the new students on . . . er . . . yes . . . on Friday night? You know, give them some info about the clubs and welfare facilities . . . and . . . oh, yes tell them about the free lectures on current affairs in the library every Tues . . . no sorry Thursday. And, don't forget . . . the disco on Wednesday . . . evening. Thanks. . . see you.

5 (See Appendix: Prescribed texts)

PAPER 3 USE OF ENGLISH (2 hours)

SECTION A

1 *Fill each of the numbered blanks in the following passage with **one** suitable word.*

Recently, there has .... (1) growing recognition that books should .... (2) a prominent part in children's lives .... (3) from babyhood. It has been shown that access to books .... (4) parents and other adults, greatly increases a child's .... (5) of becoming a happy and involved .... (6) being. The dedicated involvement of adults is, of .... (7), an essential part of the process. .... (8) this help a baby or small child has no chance at .... (9) of discovering books, or of starting on the .... (10) to that unique association with the printed word .... (11) the mature reader knows and loves. Parents need not consider this as .... (12) another onerous duty as children's books .... (13) days are things of beauty and delight. Adults .... (14) become convinced that they .... (15) share books with children present .... (16) with a passport to fun, quite .... (17) from the opportunity to stay in .... (18) with children during the years .... (19) their minds are .... (20) expanding.

2 *Finish each of the following sentences in such a way that it means exactly the same as the sentence printed before it.*

   EXAMPLE: I know he will be confused by the directions.

   ANSWER: He is *sure to be confused by the directions.*

   a) 'Why did you do it?' asked his mother.
      His mother asked him ....

   b) Unless the train arrives on time, we shall miss the start of the concert.
      If ....

   c) How did you find out where I live?
      Who ....?

   d) They all went to the seaside for the day.
      All ....

   e) Nowadays children don't learn mathematics the same way as I did.
      Nowadays children learn ....

   f) Would you like to run through your brief before the meeting?
      Do ....?

   g) The dentist said I should have the tooth out.
      The dentist advised ....

   h) Let's not give up yet.
      It would ....

3   *Fill each of the numbered blanks with a suitable word or phrase.*

EXAMPLE: When you go to America, don't *forget to write* to me.

a) Would you like to see *Starwars Part III*?
    No thanks, ... already.

b) I rarely go skiing in March unless .... good.

c) Why .... ?
    Because I was parked on double yellow lines.

d) I have to go to Cardiff tomorrow, but .... to.

e) Please turn the radio down, I'm .... sleep.

f) After a hot day's work, nothing .... a nice cool shower.

4   *For each of the sentences below, write a new sentence as similar as possible in meaning to the original sentence, but using the words given: these words must **not be altered** in any way.*

EXAMPLE: I didn't know that you could speak Arabic.
         idea
ANSWER: *I had no idea that you could speak Arabic.*

a) The entrance to the museum is over there.
    enter

    ....

b) I have no idea what this is all about.
    nothing

    ....

c) I'd rather like to go to America for a holiday.
    mind

    ....

d) Who told you there would be an election soon?
    find

    ....

e) Mr Brown is very busy; I'm afraid he can't see you.
    spare

    ....

28

f) It's no use trying to study now; it's too late.
    point

    ....

g) I can't understand what all this is about.
    comprehension

    ....

h) The meeting will be led by Mr Roberts.
    chair

    ....

5 *Read the following passage, then answer the questions which follow it.*

I tried to learn Arabic, taking a crash-course of a dozen lessons with a lovely Egyptian girl who had a voice like spring rain and a Ph.D in Linguistics. We stared solemnly at each other's uvulas; she inspecting mine to find out why it wasn't making the right noises; I inspecting hers for the sheer pleasure of looking at a piece of apparatus which
5 was capable of producing such enchanting sounds. There is a letter in Arabic, beyond the range of the English palate and the English alphabet, which is usually represented in transcription by a *9*. To make the right noise, one has to tie one's vocal cords into a sort of reef-knot, then instantly release them, so for a split second, in the middle of a word, one sounds like someone being strangled. We struggled for hours over the *9ayn*;
10 gurgling together into a tape recorder. 'It comes,' said Fatma, 'from deeper in the throat.' I never found it.

What I did discover was the pure pleasure of the Arabic alphabet. Within a few hours the mysterious dots and ripples began to sort themselves out into recognisable letters. It is an alphabet of perfect economic logic. A single little wave-shaped mark
15 does multiple service. With a dot underneath it, it is a *b*; with a dot above, it's an *n*; with two dots above it's a *t*; with three dots above it becomes a *th*-sound; and with two dots below it turns into a *y*. The strange symmetry of Arabic writing comes from using a small repertoire of intrinsically elegant shapes—uprights, ripples, waves and simple curves—and giving them identity by annotating them with a near-
20 mathematical system of dotting.

The words themselves opened the door far wider for me than I had anticipated. Each word is a tight bundle of consonants; vowels are spoken but not written. Every bundle is related to a 'root'—a key word which acts as father-figure to an extended linguistic family of words and meanings. The root-word of everything to do with
25 writing, for instance, is *ktb*—to write. By small variations on the root, one can derive the words for document, bookseller, booklet, penmanship, desk, office, library, bookshop, correspondence, dictation, novelist, typewriter, secretary, newspaper reporter, predestination (what is written as one's fate), and subscriber. It is a language of inherent, logical ambiguity. Behind every word one uses lie the ranked shadows of
30 all the other words in the family, crowding insistently in to give body and depth to the most casual utterance.

As a conversational instrument, my Arabic is useless. I am limited to greetings, street directions, words for food and thank-yous. To live in Arabic is to live in a labyrinth of false turns and double meanings. No sentence means quite what it says.
35 Every word is potentially a talisman conjuring the ghosts of the entire family of words from which it comes. The devious complexity of Arabic grammar is legendary. It is a language which is perfectly constructed for saying nothing with enormous eloquence; a language of pure manners in which there are hardly any literal meanings at all and in which symbolic gesture is everything. Arabic makes English look simple-minded, and
40 French a mere jargon of cost-accountants. Even to peer through a chink in the wall of the language is enough to glimpse the depth and darkness of that forest of ambiguity.

a) What was interesting about the writer's uvula to the Egyptian girl?

b) What was different about his reaction to her uvula?

c) Explain a 'crash-course' (line 1).

d) Explain in your own words 'a sort of reef-knot' and say why the phrase is appropriate to describe what happened to the writer's vocal chords (line 8).

e) Why was the Arabic '9ayn' difficult for the writer to pronounce?

f) Explain the phrase 'sort themselves out' (line 13).

g) What did the writer find pleasurable about the Arabic alphabet?

h) Why was it described as having 'perfect economic logic' (line 14)?

i) In what way is Arabic writing given a 'strange symmetry' (line 17)?

j) Explain the phrase 'opened the door' (line 21).

k) Explain the meaning of 'a tight bundle' (line 22).

l) What was interesting about the Arabic 'ktb' (line 25)?

m) How can a language be described as having 'logical ambiguity' (line 29)?

n) Why does the writer liken using Arabic to living in 'a labyrinth' (line 34)?

o) Summarise in 50—100 words the writer's feelings about the Arabic language.

....

....

....

....

....

....

....

....

....

....

....

PAPER 4 LISTENING COMPREHENSION (Approx. 30 minutes)

FIRST PART

For each of the questions 1—7 put a tick (√) in one of the boxes, A, B, C or D.

1 The programme 'Bric à Brac' is aimed at people who are

   A art connoisseurs.

   B amateur dealers.

   C seeking information.

   D collecting antiques.

A	
B	
C	
D	

2 According to Andrew Chambers, Mr Marshall's jugs are

   A less valuable than he thought.

   B early nineteenth-century.

   C not as old as he thought.

   D made of semi-precious metal.

A	
B	
C	
D	

3 The jugs were apparently used for

   A serving draught ale.

   B drinking beer.

   C testing the strength of the beer.

   D removing the froth from the casks.

A	
B	
C	
D	

4   The lid of the patch box which Janet sent in

    A   had a leaf design.

    B   was made of enamel.

    C   was painted blue and white.

    D   was decorated with flowers.

A	
B	
C	
D	

5   Andrew implies that society in the eighteenth century

    A   behaved abnormally.

    B   adopted affectations.

    C   despised sincerity.

    D   was naturally artful.

A	
B	
C	
D	

6   Fashionable ladies in the eighteenth century used patches to

    A   blacken their skin.

    B   darken their eyes.

    C   enhance their beauty.

    D   soften their skin.

A	
B	
C	
D	

7   The amount Janet's patch box could fetch would depend on

    A   what she hoped to get for it.

    B   the person who wanted to buy it.

    C   what she originally paid for it.

    D   whether it formed part of a collection.

A	
B	
C	
D	

SECOND PART

For each of the questions 1—4 put a tick (✓) in one of the boxes, A, B, C or D.

1   Lucy was surprised to find the foyer on level 3 as

    A   she thought it would be nearer the main entrance.

    B   the guide said it was on level 5.

    C   Terry thought it was on the administration level.

    D   she had expected it to be on level 1.

A	
B	
C	
D	

2   They decided to go and eat on level 7

    A   when they saw other people eating up there.

    B   because that's where they thought the café was.

    C   as the Cut Above restaurant is up there.

    D   because they saw a notice directing them up there.

A	
B	
C	
D	

3   They had difficulty in finding the café because

    A   the signs don't indicate where it is.

    B   none of the lifts go to that level.

    C   they weren't sure where they were.

    D   only even-numbered levels are shown in the lifts.

A	
B	
C	
D	

4   Why did Lucy and Terry go to the wrong theatre?

    A   They didn't know the name of the play.

    B   They thought *Henry IV* was on somewhere else.

    C   The sign said their play was on level 2.

    D   They didn't realise there were two theatres.

A	
B	
C	
D	

THIRD PART

For each of the questions 1—5 put a tick (√) in one of the boxes, A, B, C or D.

1   Sara speaks very hesitantly because she

    A   doesn't know what to say.

    B   finds it difficult to speak English.

    C   has problems talking to people.

    D   is frightened of the counsellor.

A	
B	
C	
D	

2   She shows that she is upset by the way she

    A   forgets the director's name.

    B   changes her mind.

    C   agrees with the counsellor.

    D   repeats everything.

A	
B	
C	
D	

3 Part of Sara's problem about communicating with others is that she

    A doesn't understand their language.

    B is in an alien culture.

    C is dominated by her family.

    D is terrified of boys.

A	
B	
C	
D	

4 What might the counsellor be thinking when Sara says she is not nervous of her?

    A 'Perhaps I can really help this girl.'

    B 'It's only because I'm a mother substitute.'

    C 'I wonder if she's going to have a breakdown.'

    D 'Whatever's the director going to say?'

A	
B	
C	
D	

5 By the end of the conversation the counsellor has managed to

    A cure Sara of her shyness.

    B remove Sara's fear of the director.

    C impress on Sara the necessity to play games.

    D persuade Sara to attend group therapy.

A	
B	
C	
D	

FOURTH PART

For questions 1 and 2 look at the timetable of the college examinations, and for question 3 the list of subjects.

Examination Timetable

Subject	Block	Room	Time
English			
	A		2·30
		3	
			2·15
	D		

Subject	
Spanish	
French	
German	
English	

1   Which block now has no examinations?

....

2   Fill in the spaces in the college examination plan.

3   Look at the list of examination subjects. Tick the box beside those which are oral.

PAPER 5 INTERVIEW (Approx. 20 minutes)

(i) *Look at this picture carefully and be prepared to answer some questions about it.*

1 Describe the scene in the picture.

2 What is the man doing?

3 Why do you think he is wearing overalls?

4 Why are the chickens in such small cages?

Battery farming
Free range v. battery eggs
Cruelty to animals

(ii)   *Look at this passage and be prepared to answer some questions about it and then to read it aloud.*

Supersports offers you and your guests a perfect and memorable way of watching the year's classic sporting events. You can enjoy them all with hospitality, luxury and prestige. Whether you have one guest or require a private facility for a large party, our options provide the widest choice, and the highest quality.

   As pioneers of luxury sporting packages, we have acquired an unrivalled range of facilities and the best seats at all the classic events. Everything is designed to ensure your absolute satisfaction. Our timing is perfect; you arrive long before the traffic and crowds converge. Soon you are relaxing among friends enjoying a welcoming drink. Your entertainment has begun—in the style that is Supersports.

SAMPLE QUESTIONS

Where might you hear this?
Who is likely to be speaking?
What is being offered?

Now read the passage aloud.

(iii)   *There may be a variety of options offered in this section. Choose one of the following:*

a)   Discussion.

   Be prepared to discuss a subject initiated by the examiner, for example:
   Literacy

   You may be invited to give your comments on various aspects, such as:
      importance for personal development
      social stigma
      necessity for developing countries

   If you are participating in a group discussion you might be asked to speak individually about one of these categories.

b)

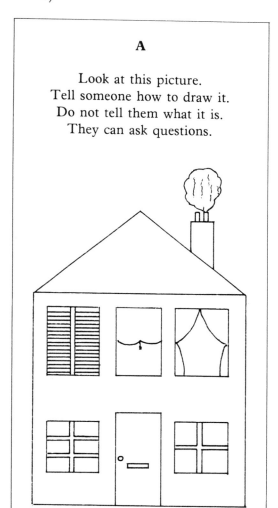

A

Look at this picture.
Tell someone how to draw it.
Do not tell them what it is.
They can ask questions.

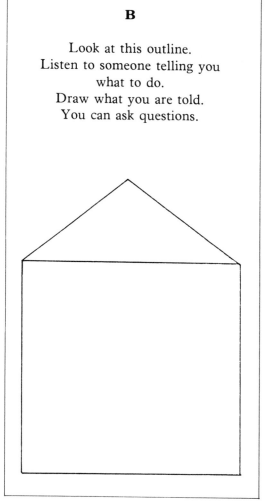

B

Look at this outline.
Listen to someone telling you
what to do.
Draw what you are told.
You can ask questions.

Compare your pictures.

(Two candidates or candidate/examiner.)

c) Prescribed texts—See Appendix.

PAPER 1 READING COMPREHENSION (1 hour)

SECTION A

*In this section you must choose the word or phrase which best completes each sentence.
Indicate the letter A, B, C or D against the number of each item 1 to 25 for the word or
phrase you choose.* **Give one answer only** *to each question.*

1 There were no .... of the Sunday papers due to a printers' strike.
A publications B volumes C editions D periodicals

2 Making colours vanish is one of this machine's .... features.
A only B unique C certain D solitary

3 He was employed as a .... man to reduce the number of workers.
A chopper B hammer C dagger D hatchet

4 If you can .... the clues to this puzzle, you could win a prize.
A unwind B unravel C unbind D untangle

5 When the bell rings in the afternoon, there is a general .... from the school.
A embarkation B migration C exodus D emigration

6 The new TV station was worried about .... revenue from advertisers.
A dwindling B waning C fading D sinking

7 Certain conditions were .... in the contract.
A put out B set out C dealt out D opened out

8 When typing it is advisable to leave a wide .... on both sides of the page.
A border B column C surround D margin

9 If your house is damp then you must .... dry rot.
A look down on B look back on C look out for D look up to

10 A role-play session is particularly useful in bringing together
different .... of teaching.
A cords B fibres C threads D strands

11 To begin the meeting, let's take an .... of the present situation.
A overview B oversight C overture D overtone

12 Refreshments at the exhibition will be available on a .... basis.
A currency B cash C money D change

13 She decided to go to lunch when she heard the town hall clock .... the hour.
    A ring   B peal   C toll   D strike

14 Unemployment·was at the .... of the problem.
    A bulb   B seed   C root   D shoot

15 I must .... that I have never visited Westminster Abbey although I live in London.
    A concede   B confirm   C confess   D confide

16 When disaster strikes, organisations .... Oxfam quickly provide help.
    A same as   B such as   C such like   D alike

17 Many bulbs flower .... the spring.
    A within   B amid   C during   D inside

18 Tommy was constantly being .... for lack of attention to his work.
    A pulled over   B pulled down   C pulled in   D pulled up

19 Although the signature tune was unpopular, the radio producer .... by his decision not to change it.
    A stayed   B stood   C kept   D held

20 I've told you .... that you cannot go out and play until you've finished your homework.
    A once and for all   B to all intents   C all the way   D in all respects

21 The anti-nuclear campaigners joined hands and formed a 20 kilometre human ....
    A chain   B link   C cable   D strand

22 I agree with you in principle; .... we should keep falling interest rates in mind.
    A moreover   B otherwise   C nevertheless   D notwithstanding

23 The money was a .... as they hadn't expected to receive anything in their aunt's will.
    A jackpot   B windfall   C hand-out   D rake-off

24 Directly he saw her, he fell .... in love.
    A from head to foot   B head over heels   C head and shoulders
    D top to toe

25 That work is needed by next week, so make sure you keep to the ....
    A deadline   B dead stop   C dead end   D deadlock

SECTION B

In this section you will find after each of the passages a number of questions or unfinished statements about the passage, each with four suggested answers or ways of finishing. You must choose the one you think fits best. Underline the letter A, B, C or D against the number of each item, 26 to 40, for the answer you choose. **Give one answer only** *to each question. Read each passage right through before choosing your answers.*

FIRST PASSAGE

A few years ago a lone American campaigner wrote a book in which he set out the main points of his fascinating crusade—to abolish television. His manifesto *Four Arguments for the Elimination of Television* is an American cult bestseller, and after eight editions is still generating concern and savage debate in the USA.

Jerry Mander, a former advertising expert is convinced that for the sake of our freedom, and mental and physical health, we should learn to live without TV. Through his advertising background Mander is aware of how much of television is concerned with advertising. He sees the planting of values for profit as 'a deep, profound and disturbing act by the few against the many, for a trivial purpose.' And, even without commercials, he sees TV as disturbing because it crams people's heads with images which alter the way they feel and behave. Pictures formed by 300,000 tiny dancing dots altering 30 times per second, bombard their eyes as people scan the images 10 times a second. The brain registers and stores all 30 images, but the conscious mind registers far fewer. But, argues Mander, even if you reject or doubt what you see consciously, it is too late, the crucial messages have gone home.

He further argues that TV is a deadening experience as it is restricted to just two senses—sight and sound. Perception is dulled and flattened says Mander, when you can't feel and smell and totally experience an event. People are just sitting passively for up to four hours a night watching a flickering screen and listening to artificial sound. 'No culture in history has spent such an enormous amount of time looking at artificial light,' says Mander, 'and another worrying fact is that prolonged exposure to artificial light alters human cells, which is why it is being used for certain medical treatment.' Researchers do not know if life-long TV exposure is a physical risk or not, but as Mander would argue, why run the risk? It is important that people get up now and switch off before the harm is done—they might also become brainwashed, or, who knows, even moribund.

26 *Four Arguments for the Elimination of Television* is a book which

    A   caused distress to many Americans.

    B   achieved great success overseas.

    C   became the 'in-book' to read.

    D   expressed the views of a fascinating man.

27 Jerry Mander objects to TV advertising mainly because

    A   the underlying principles concern money-making.

    B   it is ineffectual in getting its message across.

    C   a few people are deeply disturbed by it.

    D   the values it conveys are accepted by all.

28 Mander thinks people's feelings and behaviour are changed because

    A   the brain is able to make conscious decisions.

    B   the conscious mind is incapable of filtering images to the brain.

    C   their eyes scan a TV screen 10 times a second.

    D   the conscious mind is unable to reject the images it sees.

29 By watching TV for several hours every night, Mander implies that

    A   people would lose the use of their other senses.

    B   people's experience of life would become deadened.

    C   people's ability to respond to events would lessen.

    D   people would come to depend on only two senses.

30 Mander suggests that viewing TV over long periods of time

    A   could lead to death.

    B   might cause brain damage.

    C   could endanger people's health.

    D   would make cells malignant.

SECOND PASSAGE

In England, along a stretch of the north-east coast which gently curves from Northumberland to the estuary of the river Tees, there was a spot, typical of many on that coast, where sea-coal collected richly and effortlessly. This coal was a coarse powder, clean and brilliant like particles of crushed jet; it seemed to bear little resemblance to the large, filthy lumps put onto the fire. Although it was coal, it was perfectly clean and it was silently deposited at high tide in a glittering carpet a kilometre long for the local community to gather up.

The gear needed for sea-coaling expeditions was a curious and traditionally proven assortment which never varied from community to community along the entire north-east coastline. Sacks were essential to put the coal in, and string to tie the neck of each sack when it was full. A wooden rake was used to scrape the coal from the beach, and it was generally made from an old broom handle with a flat piece of wood nailed on at a slight reclining angle at the end. The only alternative to the rake was a flat piece of board held in the hand, which children and other ancillary workers crouched down to use. A flat, broad shovel, to lift the raked coal into the bags, completed the portable hardware.

But the most crucial item of equipment was a bicycle, a special kind of rusty, stripped-down model which was the symbol of the sea-coaling craft. A lady's bike was no good because it lacked a crossbar, and that was an essential element in transporting sea-coal. One full sack could be slung through the triangular frame of a man's bike, another over the crossbar and, sometimes, even a third on top of that. The beauty of this was that it not only enabled one to move the sea-coal from place to place, but the pressure of the metal bars against the full, wet sacks forced excess water out of the coal while it was being wheeled home. On a good day, the path to the beach was generally a double snailtrack of water that had been forced from each end of a trail of coal sacks.

31 The attraction of collecting sea-coal was that it

    A burnt better on the fire.

    B was freely available.

    C was clean and fine-grained.

    D made no noise while burning.

32 The reason certain equipment was used was because

    A the people were very traditional.

    B few communities possessed it.

    C it was shown to be practical.

    D the communities had curious habits.

33 To remove the coal from the beach, the children had to

    A bend over to use the rakes.

    B use pieces of board at reclining angles.

    C crouch down with flat shovels.

    D squat to use broad pieces of wood.

34 To carry three sacks of coal on a bicycle it was necessary to

    A lodge one of them on the saddle.

    B balance them on the crossbar.

C   balance two on the crossbar.

D   put two through the framework.

35   You could see where the coal had been transported from the beach by the

A   wet marks on the road.

B   tracks in the sand.

C   wheel marks on the path.

D   twin trails of water.

THIRD PASSAGE

Extract 1

How many calories do you need? It is estimated that the average woman burns up 2,000 calories a day; and the average man from 2,500 to 3,000 calories. Therefore if you are an overweight woman and you cut your calorie intake down to 1,500 a day, you should automatically shed weight. As a general rule, the more overweight you are, the faster you will lose it when you start dieting. But because you eat less food while you are slimming, it is important to make sure that your diet is nutritionally sound. Your daily meals should include some low-fat, protein-containing foods, plenty of vegetables and fresh fruit and some whole grain cereal foods. Weigh and measure all food accurately and remember, do not exceed your daily calorie quota.

Extract 2

Arnam knows what it is like to be hungry. His father is a casual labourer in Bangladesh who is lucky to earn £5 a month. More often than not, there is no work and little food for Arnam's family. They sometimes get milk from a voluntary agency but not on a regular basis. Arnam was two, when helpers at the agency recognised that he needed urgent nutritional help if he was to survive, so he was sent to a Save the Children unit. Here he was given treatment round the clock for starvation and the related ills. Within two days, the swelling of his face and limbs began to subside and soon he could enjoy a solid meal. His mother came in every day to be with him and to attend classes in nutrition. Teaching the mothers the right way to feed the family on what is available locally is essential if the children are not to revert to the same sorry state.

Extract 3

How many of us know what our daily nutritional needs are? How many of us, when buying food at the shop or supermarket, consider what the nutritional value of each of our purchases is? A harassed mother will rush around the supermarket, buying foods which are simple and quick to prepare. She will often buy foods which have been advertised on television or which are attractively wrapped. Mothers can be seen leaving supermarkets with trolleys piled high with 'junk foods'. Their families are eating far more calories than are good for them. Often they are over-eating on the protein side as well, by eating more meat than they need. Families spend money on food that is unnecessary or even harmful.

36 What is the importance of calories in slimming?

    A   1,500 is the maximum number anyone should use up.

    B   The number burnt up by overweight women must be greater.

    C   The number used must balance with the number taken in.

    D   The number taken in must be decreased.

37 What is the purpose of mentioning that Arnam's father is a 'casual labourer' in extract 2?

    A   It implies he is socially unimportant.

    B   It indicates a background of poverty.

    C   It shows the scarcity of work in Bangladesh.

    D   It suggests he is incapable of working regularly.

38 Extract 2 is probably taken from

    A   an educational textbook.

    B   a voluntary organisation leaflet.

    C   a propaganda pamphlet.

    D   a Third World newspaper.

39 What is the connecting theme in all three extracts?

    A   The gap between the rich and poor countries.

    B   The types of food eaten in different countries.

    C   The necessity for everyone to eat less protein.

    D   The importance of nutritional balance in food.

40 Compared with extract 3, the foods described in extract 1 appear to

    A   possess more nutritional value.

    B   show a greater variety of types.

    C   be more plentiful.

    D   contain more calories.

PAPER 2 COMPOSITION (2 hours)

*Write **two only** of the following composition exercises. Your answers must follow exactly the instructions given.*

1 Write a descriptive account of a visit to a busy city. (About 350 words)

46

2 Write a balanced discussion on the theme 'Modern technology is of benefit to everyone'. You may write in the form of a dialogue between two speakers, or in essay form. (About 350 words)

3 Describe the achievement and influence of any sportsman or sportswoman of your country. (About 200 words)

4 You return from lunch one day to find this note waiting for you. Write the letter dealing with the queries in the note. Your answer should not exceed 200 words.

Called on Brown Bros today—terrible problems about non-arrival of our promised delivery of books. Please write urgently to Managing Director, Keith Richards, explaining about delay—packers' strike, etc., and saying when he can expect the order. Do your best—this is an important customer—Bob.

5 (See Appendix: Prescribed texts)

PAPER 3   USE OF ENGLISH   (2 hours)

SECTION A

1 *Fill each of the numbered blanks in the following passage with* **one** *suitable word.*

The village has changed .... (1) in outward appearance during the last fifty years. Three of the old cottages have .... (2) and to replace .... (3) about half a dozen new pink-roofed bungalows have been .... (4). The village inn has been brought up to .... (5) and its former frontage .... (6) oak beams and cream plaster has .... (7) place to one decorated with green glazed tiles and red paint; but it is .... (8) known as the 'Magpie' and the old signboard with .... (9) knowing bird .... (10) a gold ring in its beak still .... (11) in its old position .... (12) the inn door. The old lollipop shop with bull's-eyes and barley sugar .... (13) its dim green bottle-glass window has .... (14) the General Stores. .... (15) one of its walls a scarlet Post .... (16) letterbox has appeared .... (17) a notice above it .... (18) that stamps may be .... (19) and parcels posted .... (20).

2 *Finish each of the following sentences in such a way that it means exactly the same as the sentence printed before it.*

EXAMPLE: I saw him slowly begin to understand.

ANSWER: I saw that *he slowly began to understand.*

a) 'Please don't leave me', he said to her.
   He begged ....

b) In spite of his lack of experience, he got the job.
Although..

c) From the information I've got, the plane should land at 10.
According to..

d) The organisers proposed to cancel the conference.
The organisers considered..

e) Be careful not to drop the eggs!
Whatever..

f) Stopping smoking improved my health.
My health..

g) What are your feelings about the arms race?
How...?

h) It's been so long since I last saw you.
It's been such..

3 *Fill each of the numbered blanks with a suitable word or phrase.*

EXAMPLE: As I'd only seen him once before *I couldn't remember* what he looked
like.

a) Why do you want to go to Turkey?
.... before.

b) You .... but I have known you make the odd mistake.

c) .... ?
It's John's car, I think.

d) I've only had this radio a week and it's broken already.
Why .... back?

e) I've got a terrible pain in my stomach.
If .... to the doctor's.

f) He went to the football match .... his team.

4 *For each of the sentences below, write a new sentence as similar as possible in meaning
to the original sentence, but using the words given: these words must **not be altered**
in any way.*

EXAMPLE: He wasn't allowed to see the contract.

let

Nobody would let him see the contract.

48

a) Must I really sign the form twice?
    essential

    ....

b) I can't bear the thought of nuclear war.
    unthinkable

    ....

c) He wrote down everything he did in his diary.
    record

    ....

d) She's always very helpful to everyone.
    assist

    ....

e) As well as her normal salary, she made some money by babysitting.
    supplement

    ....

f) The missing money wasn't mentioned.
    said

    ....

g) I'll give you £5 for the whole lot.
    all

    ....

h) Some people consider liberty as more important than anything else.
    free

    ....

SECTION B

5   *Read the following passage, then answer the questions which follow it.*

Once I worked as a clerk in an office and I grew thinner and my suits fell to bits and I
watched the seagulls out of the window. The months passed and I knew I had taken
the wrong road. 'You're not paid to watch seagulls,' said the manager. In my spare
time I went to Victoria station and bought cups of tea and watched the trains. The
5 ceiling of the station shook with the thunder of wheels, and there was a faint imported
smell of the sea, a catch in the throat, a volley of shouts, and an explosion of children
like fireworks. But all that mattered to me was the gold and blue of the places they had
been to, the singing names, like Leman, Maggiore, Garda, Ischia, Ibiza.
   Eventually I joined a travel agency. I almost lived in trains, pushing hordes of

people round monuments, cramming them into cathedrals, and winkling them out of gondolas. Once on the Paris−Vallorbe run, my train split in two. Half my clients disappeared down a gradient. The runaway carriages reappeared half an hour later at Vallorbe station and were greeted by hysterical shouts, as though they had come back from Siberia. But the train didn't pull up. It puffed off busily in the general direction of Italy, and I found it quite impossible to control the pandemonium on the station platform. Even I, the courier, wasn't aware that this divided train was returning to another platform.

    I lived in a world of smoke, station buffets, customs offices and rattling corridors; the antiseptic rush through the Simplon tunnel; the gleaming run beside the lake of Geneva; carriages of priests, soldiers, Chianti and garlic between Pisa and Rome; and the eternal solid caravan of British clients getting constipated from pasta and ruins. I was still a prisoner entangled in a web of questions, complaints and prejudices. But through the carriage window, past the vacuum flask and the knitting needles, I could see the running rainbow feet of beauty.

    After a time I began to weary of trains and to long for London. But I could not escape. The demon that had haunted me in the office and dragged me to Victoria station to gape at the expresses would not release me. It was my living. Sleeping past Lyons, breakfast at the frontier, loving past Stresa, eating past the Apennines. Eventually I broke up a highly organised tour of Italy by running off with one of the clients, was sacked by the agency and took up writing.

    a) How do we know that the writer was unhappy as a clerk in an office?

    b) What does the writer mean by the phrase 'taken the wrong road' (lines 2−3)?

    c) Suggest three things that were exciting about watching the trains at Victoria station.

    d) Why should the children be said to be like an explosion of 'fireworks' (line 7)?

    e) The writer thought certain places had 'singing names'. Why should he think this?

    f) Explain in your own words 'winkling them out' (line 10).

g) What happened at Vallorbe station?

h) Why should the thought of Siberia cause 'hysterical shouts' (line 13)?

i) What is meant by 'pandemonium on the station platform' (lines 15 – 16)?

j) Explain the phrase 'antiseptic rush' in connection with the Simplon tunnel (line 19).

k) Why should the British clients be 'constipated from pasta and ruins' (line 21)?

l) Why does the writer describe the train wheels as 'the running rainbow feet of beauty' (line 24)?

m) What was 'the demon' that had haunted the writer in the office (line 26)?

n) How did the writer eventually find 'release' from the demon?

o) Summarise in 50—100 words the writer's love for trains and where it led him.

PAPER 4 LISTENING COMPREHENSION (Approx. 30 minutes)

FIRST PART

For questions 1—5 fill in the information on the university entrance requirements form (some has been filled in for you). For each of the questions 6—9 put a tick (√) in one of the boxes A, B, C or D.

⊕ University Entrance
Intake 1984/5

	University entrance requirements	Business studies and Spanish course	General entry
1	O level	5 or 4	
2	English language		Yes
3	Maths	Yes	
4	A level	2 or 3	
5	Spanish		No

6 When the student phones the university registry she discovers

   A she has the wrong combination of subjects.

   B the university doesn't offer the degree she wants.

   C a foreign language is necessary at A level.

   D she should have A level business administration.

A	
B	
C	
D	

7 What does the Universities Central Council on Admissions do?

   A Chooses universities for the students.

   B Acts as a link between students and universities.

   C Selects the right courses for students.

   D Submits reports on students to the universities.

A	
B	
C	
D	

52

8   If the student decides to read for the business studies and Spanish degree, she will have to

    A   spend four years studying Spanish business.

    B   study business in a Spanish university.

    C   live four years in a Spanish-speaking country.

    D   study abroad for part of the course.

A	
B	
C	
D	

9   The student had to apply straightaway because

    A   the universities never considered late applications.

    B   those applying late had a limited choice of universities.

    C   only a small range of subjects was offered to late applicants.

    D   she wanted to study an unusual combination of subjects.

A	
B	
C	
D	

SECOND PART

For each of the questions 1—5 put a tick (✓) in one of the boxes A, B, C or D.

1   It is difficult for travelling salesmen to

    A   find the right place to eat.

    B   keep a check on their weight.

    C   weigh their dietary needs.

    D   eat the right food.

A	
B	
C	
D	

2   How much of our daily food should be carbohydrate?

    A   50%

    B   25%

    C   2 kilos

    D   90—100 g

A	
B	
C	
D	

3   How much protein does a woman who weighs 58 kilos need daily?

    A   More than 58 g.

    B   Less than 58 g.

    C   About 60 g.

    D   At least 70 g.

A	
B	
C	
D	

4 According to the dietician, root vegetables are

    A full of protein.

    B considered fattening.

    C a rich source of fat.

    D a source of carbohydrates.

A	
B	
C	
D	

5 Which of these foods is rich in vitamin B?

    A Oranges.

    B Liver.

    C Butter.

    D Fish-liver oil.

A	
B	
C	
D	

THIRD PART

For each of the questions 1—4 put a tick (✓) in one of the boxes A, B, C or D.

1   Why does Chris suggest Women's Lib. has something to do with Sue's life expectancy?

   A   He thinks someone from Women's Lib. wrote the quiz.

   B   He wants to see what Sue will do if teased.

   C   He hopes to make Sue lose her temper with him.

   D   He believes the quiz is biased towards women.

A	
B	
C	
D	

2   Sue tells Chris he won't score any points for intelligence because

   A   she thinks he is conceited enough already.

   B   she is doubtful if he is above average.

   C   she wants to get her own back on him.

   D   she really thinks he is below average.

A	
B	
C	
D	

3   It seems the most important factor in longevity is

   A   abstention from heavy smoking.

   B   regular moderate drinking.

   C   long-living relatives.

   D   involvement in higher education.

A	
B	
C	
D	

4   By the end of the quiz it is probable that

   A   Chris will live the longest.

   B   neither of them will reach 70.

   C   both of them will live to 80.

   D   Sue will live longer than Chris.

A	
B	
C	
D	

FOURTH PART

For questions 1 and 2 look at the policy chart, and for question 3 the list of reasons for discrimination.

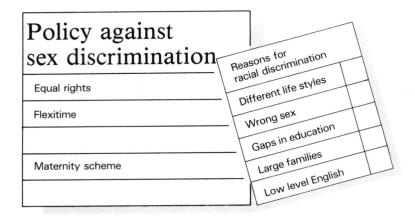

Policy against sex discrimination	
Equal rights	
Flexitime	
Maternity scheme	

Reasons for racial discrimination	
Different life styles	
Wrong sex	
Gaps in education	
Large families	
Low level English	

1   Fill in the two spaces in the policy chart above.

2   Which of the items in the policy applies to all employees, not just women? ....

3   Look at the list of reasons for racial discrimination. Tick the boxes beside those items which might cause prejudice against ethnic minorities.

PAPER 5 INTERVIEW (Approx. 20 minutes)

(i) *Look at this picture carefully and be prepared to answer some questions about it.*

1 Why are the people in the picture marching?

2 What is the purpose of the banners?

3 Why do you think most of the marchers are men?

4 Why are there a lot of policemen walking with them?

Unemployment
Changing work patterns
Right to work v. Right to leisure

(ii) *Look at this passage and be prepared to answer some questions about it and then to read it aloud.*

May I offer a warm welcome to you all. Many of you, I know, have travelled a long way to be with us tonight and everyone here appreciates the efforts you have made. Well, we have a very mixed bag of items up for discussion, some of which may cause a degree of controversy, so I won't stand on ceremony but just dip into the pile and see what comes up first. Ah, well this should get the ball rolling and start a few sparks flying, so may I throw it to you first, Jack Straw, to get your reactions. Remember, the panel can be questioned on their opinions at any time after a member has finished speaking, but please, do not interrupt during a speech. Right, here goes . . .

SAMPLE QUESTIONS

Who is probably speaking here?
What is the situation?
Where might it be taking place?

Now read the passage aloud.

(iii) *There may be a variety of options offered in this section. Choose one of the following:*

a) Discussion.

Be prepared to discuss a subject initiated by the examiner,
for example: **Conservation**

You may be invited to give your comments on various aspects, such as:
disposal of waste materials
economic use of energy resources
preservation of the countryside

If you are participating in a group discussion you might be asked to speak individually about one of these categories.

b) You arrive at your school/college one morning and find this notice. Consider what you will say to a member of the staff you meet later.

Staff Strike!

As from 10 o'clock this morning, all staff will be on strike for higher salaries. Any inconvenience caused to students is regretted but the English Course will not be resumed until a settlement is reached.

(Examiner takes the part of the member of staff.)

c) Prescribed texts—See Appendix.

Test Four

PAPER 1   READING COMPREHENSION   (1 hour)

SECTION A

In this section you must choose the word or phrase which best completes each sentence.
Indicate the letter A, B, C or D against the number of each item 1 to 25 for the word or
phrase you choose. **Give one answer only** *to each question.*

1   The illustrator, Aubrey Beardsley, ... the imagination of succeeding
    generations of artists.
    A raised   B heated   C fired   D burnt

2   I wish you wouldn't .... me, I'm doing my best.
    A keep at it   B keep on with   C keep up with   D keep on at

3   Many people still live in bleak .... city areas.
    A inward   B internal   C inner   D interior

4   Please fill in the questionnaire and return it to the market .... agents.
    A research   B enquiry   C investigation   D information

5   The doorway was so low that he had to .... his head down to enter.
    A stoop   B bow   C bend   D drop

6   The windows were .... high up in the walls of the castle.
    A set   B fixed   C seated   D settled

7   From the woods a winding path .... down to the seashore.
    A wavered   B coiled   C rolled   D meandered

8   A traditional English breakfast consisted of at least two eggs and
    several .... of bacon.
    A slices   B rashers   C slivers   D strips

9   He is very generous with his money, he's always ....
    A open-hearted   B open-mouthed   C open-minded   D open-handed

10 Even .... she speaks well, she doesn't communicate.
    A despite   B so   C though   D that

11 The overweight man became wedged in the exhibition .... as he tried to
    enter.
    A enclosure   B turnstile   C barrier   D barricade

12 Really, that child .... the most extraordinary language.

A comes out with   B comes down on   C comes in for   D comes out of

13 When you buy a house in England you can claim tax .... on the mortgage.

A aid   B assistance   C relief   D benefit

14 The police said there was no sign of a .... entry even though the house had been burgled.

A forced   B smashed   C broken   D burst

15 To order the goods, send your name, address and .... to the following PO box.

A cost   B remittance   C settlement   D receipt

16 The trouble with cats and dogs is that their hair comes out in the spring when they ....

A peel   B cast   C shed   D moult

17 He wasn't very sure of the committee's reaction, so he approached the matter rather ....

A stealthily   B diligently   C gingerly   D thoroughly

18 Although many people have doubts about new technology, ... it will probably benefit mankind.

A in good time   B in the event   C in the long run   D as a result

19 As well as answering the questions, you have to complete a .... to win the competition in the event of a draw.

A vexed question   B tie breaker   C knotty problem   D sealed book

20 Having decided to take the examination, you might .... make an effort to study.

A just a bit   B in part   C more or less   D at least

21 Newly printed newspapers often .... a strange smell.

A give off   B give away   C give over   D give up

22 Broadcasting companies are .... evaluating stereo transmissions for television.

A lately   B presently   C recently   D currently

23 The train came to .... halt at the level crossing as the gates closed unexpectedly.

A a headlong   B a rushed   C an abrupt   D a prompt

24 His first commercial venture was selling self-assembly .... for miniature
    radios.
    A outfits   B kits   C fittings   D units

25 With great determination, successful people often achieve the ....
    A impossible   B inconceivable   C unlikely   D unimaginable

SECTION B

*In this section you will find after each of the passages a number of questions or unfinished
statements about the passage, each with four suggested answers or ways of finishing. You
must choose the one you think fits best. Underline the letter A, B, C or D against the
number of each item, 26 to 40, for the answer you choose. **Give one answer only** to
each question. Read each passage right through before choosing your answers.*

FIRST PASSAGE

Recent research has claimed that an excess of positive ions in the air can have an ill-effect
on people's physical or psychological health. What are positive ions? Well, the air is full
of ions, electrically charged particles, and generally there is a rough balance between the
positive and the negative charged. But sometimes this balance becomes disturbed and a
larger proportion of positive ions are found. This happens naturally before
thunderstorms, earthquakes or when winds such as the Mistral, Foehn, Hamsin or
Sharav are blowing in certain countries. Or it can be caused by a build-up of static
electricity indoors from carpets or clothing made of man-made fibres, or from TV sets,
duplicators or computer display screens.

When a large number of positive ions are present in the air many people experience
unpleasant effects such as headaches, fatigue, irritability, and some particularly sensitive
people suffer nausea or even mental disturbance. Animals are also found to be affected,
particularly before earthquakes; snakes have been observed to come out of hibernation,
rats to flee from their burrows, dogs howl and cats jump about unaccountably. This has
led the US Geographical Survey to fund a network of volunteers to watch animals in an
effort to foresee such disasters before they hit vulnerable areas such as California.

Conversely, when large numbers of negative ions are present, then people have a
feeling of well-being. Natural conditions that produce these large amounts are near the
sea, close to waterfalls or fountains, or in any place where water is sprayed, or forms a
spray. This probably accounts for the beneficial effect of a holiday by the sea, or in the
mountains with tumbling streams or waterfalls.

To increase the supply of negative ions indoors, some scientists recommend the use of
ionisers: small portable machines which generate negative ions. They claim that ionisers
not only clean and refresh the air but also improve the health of people sensitive to excess
positive ions. Of course, there are the detractors, other scientists, who dismiss such
claims and are sceptical about negative/positive ion research. Therefore people can only
make up their own minds by observing the effects on themselves, or on others, of a
negative rich or poor environment. After all, it is debatable whether depending on seismic
readings to anticipate earthquakes is more effective than watching the cat.

26 What effect does excessive positive ionisation have on some people?
    A They think they are insane.
    B They feel rather bad-tempered.
    C They become violently sick.
    D They are too tired to do anything.

27 According to the passage, static electricity can be caused by
    A using home-made electrical goods.
    B wearing clothes made of natural materials.
    C walking on artificial floor coverings.
    D copying TV programmes on a computer.

28 By observing the behaviour of animals, scientists may be able to
    A prevent disasters.
    B organise groups of people.
    C predict earthquakes.
    D control areas of California.

29 A high negative ion count is likely to be found
    A near a pond with a water pump.
    B close to a slow-flowing river.
    C high in some barren mountains.
    D by a rotating water sprinkler.

30 People should be able to come to a decision about ions in the air if they
    A note their own reactions.
    B move to a healthier area.
    C observe domestic animals.
    D watch how wealthy people behave.

SECOND PASSAGE

You might think that the world no longer believes in demons or magic symbols. But are you sure? Consider military regiments, they have mascots, often a goat or a horse, while ships' captains still believe having a cat on board will bring luck.

Certain symbols have a very ancient ancestry; the swastika, for example, is an ancient sign brought to Europe by the Crusaders from the Saracens in the Middle Ages. It signified the movement of the seasons, and used to appear on horse brasses along with stars, circles, crescents and other protective symbols. In the Second World War a clockwise swastika was adopted by Adolf Hitler as the Nazi symbol—Hitler was extremely superstitious and believed in the swastika's lucky power, rather misguidedly as it turned out.

Corn dollies, made from the last sheaf of corn cut, are still popular in countries as far apart as Mexico, the Balinese Islands and Great Britain. Originally they were a means of encouraging pagan gods to provide a good harvest the following year; now they are just hung up as a decoration in the kitchen, but perhaps some of the old powerful meaning attached to them is dimly remembered.

The peasants in southern China when working on their harvests used to wear special dresses. The patterned border on these always had two broad bands, representing rivers enclosing lands, and numerous squares represented fields, each with a different pattern symbolising a particular crop. In this way the peasants indicated to their gods what was expected in each field. These dresses nowadays are worn for festivals and ceremonies connected with agriculture—so the original symbolism is not forgotten. Another superstition of the Chinese was that demons fly in straight lines, hence all the important public buildings in China have curved corners to confuse the demons and prevent them from getting a hold as they fly past. For the same reason, the paths up to Chinese front doors are winding, and the doors are painted a 'demon-defying' red as an added protection.

To find some kind of protection against the power of demons has always been of importance, and all over the world certain strange customs evolved. In Asia and Europe, because baby boys were always valued above girls, the curious habit of dressing boys as girls to trick the demons occurred. Even in Victorian Britain boys wore dresses until they were about seven years old. Nowadays, girls and boys both wear jeans so perhaps the demons are still being confused.

31 The author's mention of animals, such as goats, horses or cats, is meant to show
    A   how superstitious people were in the past.
    B   the ignorance of the army and merchant navy.
    C   an example of present-day superstition.
    D   the necessity of having a mascot for luck.

32 Hitler's faith in the power of the swastika was misguided because it
    A   only offered protection to horses.
    B   possessed symbolic meaning only.
    C   was ineffective facing the wrong way.
    D   had only a seasonal use.

33 The continued use of corn dollies seems to indicate mankind's
    A   dependence on agricultural symbols.
    B   need to be surrounded by decoration.
    C   continued belief in ancient gods.
    D   desire to keep a link with the past.

34 Crops were represented in the Chinese peasant's dresses by
    A   an abstract design.
    B   a varied pattern.
    C   a chequered effect.
    D   some wide stripes.

35 The information in the passage suggests that demons
    A   were deceived by outward appearances.
    B   thought all children looked the same.
    C   couldn't tell the difference between the sexes.
    D   only attacked boys under seven years old.

THIRD PASSAGE

Extract 1
This was a typical nineteenth-century garden: a lawn stretching south from the drawing room windows, with here and there a tall specimen tree or shrub; near the house, flowerbeds with standard roses, and fancy metalwork baskets planted out with geraniums; between the lawn and the house, a hedge with a pair of urns in stone, and a couple of wide stone or brick steps leading to the lawn. To right and left, thick shrubberies, through which wound serpentine paths with here and there a rustic seat. Somewhere there would be a walled garden for fruit and vegetables, with broad borders of perennial flowers.

Extract 2
A garden should work as an extension of the house both practically and visually. While the form the garden takes evolves primarily from its function, the style above all must be in sympathy with its location. Very occasionally a contrast in style can work by shock tactics, but in the main this is not a good idea. The first problem is to recognise your style. For those who live in an old period house there is no difficulty, but for the vast majority who live in modern suburban houses it is more tricky. As a starting point give some thought to building materials, then to the interior style of the house itself. In planning your garden try above all to avoid mixing materials and styles as it is rarely successful.

Extract 3
The earliest recorded gardens, seen in Egypt about 3000 B.C., were surrounded by a mud wall to absorb some of the sun's heat. The house was also inside this square or rectangular enclosure. The formal layout of early gardens was necessitated by the need for irrigation channels to provide water in a hot, dry climate. These divided the garden into geometric areas and, in the grander gardens, the irrigation channels became formal pools with fish, and there were arbours to sit under, overhung with vines, and shade-giving palms. The Egyptians grew onions, which were their staple diet, and other vegetables and herbs for their medicinal value.

36 Why are the paths described as 'serpentine' in extract 1?
    A It indicates their curving, twisting appearance.
    B It shows they have snake-like qualities.
    C It suggests the garden might be dangerous.
    D It implies they were made with patterned materials.

37 Why is the style of a garden in extract 2 so important?
    A It gives a feeling of spaciousness.
    B It complements the surrounding countryside.
    C It provides a sense of harmony.
    D It expands the function of the house.

38 Extract 2 is probably taken from
   A a gardening catalogue.
   B a naturalist's journal.
   C a technical magazine.
   D a designer's manual.

39 Extracts 1 and 3 are about
   A attractive garden schemes.
   B how gardens are planned.
   C unusual methods of gardening.
   D different styles of gardening.

40 Compared with extract 1 the garden described in extract 3 appears to
   A contain more flowers and plants.
   B have a more symmetrical style.
   C be more romantic in design.
   D possess a greater number of objects.

PAPER 2 COMPOSITION (2 hours)

*Write **two only** of the following composition exercises. Your answers must follow exactly the instructions given.*

1 Write a descriptive account of a picnic in the country. (About 350 words)

2 Write a balanced discussion on the theme 'The most important learning takes place before the age of five'. You may write in the form of a dialogue between two speakers, or in essay form. (About 350 words)

3 Describe the importance and influence of any book you have read.
   (About 200 words)

4 You have received the following critical letter. Write a statement to be broadcast by your local radio station refuting the allegations made against you. Your answer should not exceed 200 words.

   You are the most deceitful, scheming person ever to walk the earth. Thousands of innocent people like myself heard you on the radio the other day enthusing about the latest drug your company has produced. But what about all your other products that have had terrible side-effects—sometimes resulting in death? It is disgraceful that you should put people's lives at risk for profit. But I don't expect you will have the decency to reply to my letter publicly.

5 (See Appendix: Prescribed texts)

PAPER 3 USE OF ENGLISH (2 hours)

SECTION A

1 *Fill each of the numbered blanks in the following passage with* **one** *suitable word.*

For a _____ (1) of reasons my images of Italy _____ (2) to be dominated by _____ (3) of roads and the journeys I have made _____ (4) them. The wide autostradas, major highways _____ (5) sweep majestically across the landscape as _____ (6) to demonstrate that the Italians of _____ (7) know as much _____ (8) road building as their Roman ancestors. _____ (9) there are the minor roads which keep to the _____ (10) of the trees as they venture from one small town to _____ (11). They hug the mountain _____ (12) and river banks, and wander _____ (13) the villages, swinging around so as _____ (14) to miss the best views.

I am not the _____ (15) enthusiast for the Italian highway system. Charles Dickens wrote, 'There is _____ (16) in Italy more beautiful to me _____ (17) the coast road between Genoa and Spezia' and, though the _____ (18) of a century has considerably altered the road, _____ (19) is easy to understand why he was _____ (20) attracted to that pleasant stretch of coastline.

2 *Finish each of the following sentences in such a way that it means exactly the same as the sentence printed before it.*

EXAMPLE: Ms Robinson is said to be a very good teacher.

ANSWER: Ms Robinson is regarded *as a very good teacher.*

a) Smoking can cause damage to your health.
   Your health _____

b) There is no possibility of him passing the examination.
   It is _____

c) 'Please have your passports ready', the official said to the passengers.
   The official requested _____

d) Most of the letters sent to the magazine were about nuclear war.
   Nuclear war _____

e) I can't remember where you said the cinema was.
   Where _____ ?

f) Despite having to pay high taxes, he didn't complain.
   Although _____

g) All the shops are closed this afternoon.
None ....

h) She dances more gracefully than her friend.
She is a ....

3 *Fill each of the numbered blanks with a suitable word or phrase.*

> EXAMPLE: Although I went to the airport on the off chance, *I managed to get a seat* on the plane.

a) I've always wanted a Siamese cat. Wouldn't .... one?

b) The more I see him, ... him.

c) Why .... ?
I want to see the manager.

d) I wouldn't have bothered to ask you if I .... the answer.

e) Whenever I have tried to learn German, something ....

f) Unless you read the instructions you .... idea of what to do.

4 *For each of the sentences below, write a new sentence as similar as possible in meaning to the original sentence, but using the words given: these words must **not be altered** in any way.*

> EXAMPLE: His affection for her never changed.
> **constant**
>
> ANSWER: *He was constant in his affection for her.*

a) He imitates people very well.
impressionist

....

b) Tell me where you would like to eat.
indication

....

c) It was highly unlikely that Maria knew the answer.
possibility

....

d) The manager was extremely annoyed at the inefficiency of the staff.
anger

....

e) She was very upset by the death of her cat.
tears

....

f) Do you recollect seeing Timothy in Paris last year?
memory

....

g) The audacity of his reply took my breath away.
left

....

h) There just isn't enough room in here for another table.
small

....

SECTION B

5 *Read the following passage, then answer the questions which follow it.*

Friday 27 August

Today I paid my first visit to Stonehenge. We had breakfast before church and immediately after service Morris and I started to walk to Stonehenge, 17 kilometres. We walked through the meadows towards Salisbury with the great spire ever before us pointing heavenward. Passing through the beautiful cathedral close and the city of
5 Salisbury we took the Devizes road for some 9 kilometres and then we saw in the dim distance the mysterious stones standing upon the plain. We pushed on to the clump of trees which sheltered the Druid's Head Inn from the south-west winds and had a merry lunch in a long dark parlour adorned with a large painting of a druid's head. Then we struck across the plain eastwards and soon came in sight of the grey cluster
10 of gigantic stones. They stood in the midst of the green plain and the first impression they left in my mind was that of a group of people standing about and talking together. It seemed to me as if they were ancient giants who suddenly became silent and stiffened into stone directly anyone approached, but who might at any moment become alive again, and at certain seasons, as at midnight and on Christmas and
15 Midsummer's Eve, might circle on the plain in a solemn and stately giant's dance.
It is a solemn, awful place. As I entered the charmed circle of the sombre stones I instinctively uncovered my head, it was like entering a great cathedral church. A great silent service was going on and the stones inaudibly whispered to each other the grand secret. The sun was present at the service in his temple and the place was filled with
20 his glory. During the service we sat under the shadow of the great leaning stone upon the vast monolith which had fallen upon and crushed and which now nearly covers the altar stone. Many stones still stood upright, one leaned forward towards the east,

as if bowing to the rising sun, while some had fallen flat on their faces.

It must be a solemn thing to pass a night among the silent shadows of the awful
25 stones, to see the sun leave his temple in the evening with a farewell smile, and to
watch for him again until in the morning he enters once more by the great eastern gate
and takes his seat upon the altar stone.

As we went down the southern slope of the green plain we left the stones standing
on the hill against the sky, seeming by turns to be the enchanted giants, the silent
30 preachers, the sleepless watchers, the great cathedral on the plain.

a) Why do you think the writer had breakfast before going to church?

b) Why is the spire said to be 'pointing heavenward' (line 4)?

c) For what reason can the stones only be seen in the 'dim distance'?

d) Suggest a reason why the stones should remind the writer of people.

e) Explain the phrase 'circle on the plain' (line 15).

f) Explain the use of 'stately' in connection with a giant's dance (line 15).

g) Explain in other words 'uncovered my head' (line 17).

h) Why should the stone circle be like a 'cathedral church' (line 17)?.

i) What is meant by 'the stones inaudibly whispered to each other'
(line 18)?

j) And what could be meant by 'the grand secret' (lines 18–19)?

k) In what way was the stone circle the 'temple' of the sun (line 19)?

l) Why should the sun be personified, with the temple referred to as 'his'?

m) Why should a stone appear to be 'bowing to the rising sun' (line 23)?

....

n) In what way could the sun appear to enter the circle 'by the great eastern gate' and take 'his seat upon the altar stone' (lines 26–7)?

....

o) Summarise in 50—100 words the appearance of Stonehenge, and the effect it had upon the writer.

....

....

....

....

....

....

....

....

....

PAPER 4 LISTENING COMPREHENSION (Approx. 30 minutes)

FIRST PART

For questions 1—6, fill in the career qualifications on the form below (some have been filled in for you). For each of the questions 7—10 put a tick (✓) in one of the boxes A, B, C or D.

CONDOR AIRWAYS

AIR CONDOR HOUSE
ST STEVENS AVENUE
LONDON   SW1A 5BR

CABIN CREW/PILOT QUALIFICATIONS

		Cabin crew	Pilots
1	Age	over 18	
2	Marital status		—
3	Education		2 A levels
4	Subjects	foreign language	
5	Physical attributes		excellent eyesight
6	Personality	/unflappable	/decisive

7 Why is it necessary for members of the cabin crew to have calm personalities?

A   They have to endure a great deal of stress.

B   They frequently have to deal with medical emergencies.

C   They have to accept responsibility for the aircraft.

D   They have to set a good example to the passengers.

A
B
C
D

8 The job of stewardess or steward involves one of the following:

A   very long hours.

B   a good salary.

C   the chance of promotion.

D   hard physical work.

A
B
C
D

9 To become a successful pilot, you must

    A have at least A levels in physics and mechanics.

    B train for a further 3 years after getting your licence.

    C undertake 100 hours of ground-based flying practice.

    D spend 18 months practising elementary flying.

A	
B	
C	
D	

10 What is the first step you should take in applying for training with Condor Airways?

    A Phone the College of Air Training.

    B Obtain the address from the training officer.

    C Write to all the airline personnel departments.

    D Go to your college careers teacher.

A	
B	
C	
D	

SECOND PART

For each of the questions 1—4 put a tick (✓) in one of the boxes A, B, C or D.

1 Maria rejects the idea of taking her parents to the polytech canteen for lunch because

    A it doesn't have the right atmosphere.

    B they don't like English food.

    C only students are allowed to eat there.

    D they always eat in expensive places.

A	
B	
C	
D	

2 What is it about the Hungarian restaurant that interests Maria?

    A It serves very good quality food.

    B Many important people eat there.

    C It is out of the ordinary.

    D It's been open for 43 years.

A	
B	
C	
D	

3 One of the drawbacks of the restaurant is that it

    A only accepts cash.

    B has an unlucky number of tables.

    C is in a remote part of London.

    D is limited for space.

A	
B	
C	
D	

4   Which of the following best describes the Hungarian restaurant?

    A   Small and expensive.

    B   Discreet and pricey.

    C   Comfortable and cheap.

    D   Reasonably-priced and quiet.

A	
B	
C	
D	

THIRD PART

For each of the questions 1—3 put a tick (✓) in one of the boxes A, B, C or D.

1   The salesman shows he doesn't believe the customer by the way he

    A   is not particularly civil.

    B   keeps apologising.

    C   gets very annoyed.

    D   repeats his questions.

A	
B	
C	
D	

2   The customer becomes aggressive when he

    A   realises the salesman is talking nonsense.

    B   thinks the salesman has insulted him.

    C   perceives the salesman is a fool.

    D   feels he's getting the upper hand.

A	
B	
C	
D	

3   By the end of the conversation, the salesman has

    A   lost his temper.

    B   become abusive.

    C   met his match.

    D   gained control.

A	
B	
C	
D	

FOURTH PART

For question 1 look at the football match programme and put a tick in the correct boxes.
For each of the questions 2—4 put a tick (√) in one of the boxes A, B, C or D.

1 Where will these teams be playing tomorrow?

Teams	Grounds		
	Tottenham	Wembley	Fulham
Leeds United			
Manchester United			
Brighton			
Fulham			
Chelsea			
Tottenham			

FOOTBALL PROGRAMME

Sports Roundup

2 What time is the Willoughby Handicap at Cheltenham?

A 2.15

B 2.50

C 3.15

D 2.00

A	
B	
C	
D	

3 What kind of sporting event is taking place at the Albert Hall tomorrow?

A Wrestling.

B Boxing.

C Weight-lifting.

D Judo.

A	
B	
C	
D	

4 Who is the present title-holder?

A Joe Busby.

B Roddy Bellows.

C Toni Tortello.

D Klaus Schmidt.

A	
B	
C	
D	

PAPER 5 INTERVIEW (Approx. 20 minutes)

(i) *Look at this picture carefully and be prepared to answer some questions about it.*

1 What are these children doing?

2 What equipment are they using?

3 What kind of programme are they using?

4 Where are they probably?

Microcomputers
Young children and modern technology
Changing teaching/learning methods

(ii) *Look at this passage and be prepared to answer some questions about it and then to read it aloud.*

Travel with us and you will find there's no fuss; no long waits; no tedious queueing. Check-in is just half an hour before your flight time, and when your flight is called, you just hand in your ticket and drive onto the spacious car-deck. As you park you will be met by a stewardess who will show you to the passenger cabin where everyone, including children, gets a roomy, airline-type seat. Loading the craft only takes a few minutes and then you're up and away. During the flight your cabin staff will take orders for drinks and duty-free goods, a list of which you will find on the seat-back in front of you. These will be brought right to your seat, so just relax and enjoy the flight.

Then just 35 minutes later, you've arrived. The staff will guide you swiftly to customs and passport control and then you just drive off and resume your journey, fresh and relaxed. This is why more than 2 million people a year choose to travel with us.

SAMPLE QUESTIONS

What information is being given here?
Who is probably giving it?
What in particular is being offered?

Now read the passage aloud.

(iii) *There may be a variety of options offered in this section. Choose one of the following:*

a) Discussion.

Be prepared to discuss a subject initiated by the examiner, for example:
The nuclear arms race

You may be invited to give your comments on various aspects, such as:
the case for disarmament
international co-operation
the value of protest

If you are participating in a group discussion you might be asked to speak individually about one of these categories.

b) There are 3 men, David, Terry and Paul. Each man has 2 jobs. The 6 jobs are:

magician   pop star
barman   racing driver
pilot   disc jockey

Find out which jobs each man has, using the following information:

1 David won money from both Terry and the disc jockey at poker.

2 Terry owes the pop star £5.

3 The disc jockey often leaves the racing driver a tip.

4 The pilot goes out with the disc jockey's sister.

5 Both the pop star and the racing driver go racing with Paul.

6 The racing driver's girlfriend wants to meet the pilot.

(Explain to the examiner how you reached your decision.)

c) Prescribed texts—See Appendix.

Test Five

PAPER 1 READING COMPREHENSION (1 hour)

SECTION A

In this section you must choose the word or phrase which best completes each sentence. Indicate the letter A, B, C or D against the number of each item 1 to 25 for the word or phrase you choose. **Give one answer only** *to each question.*

1 Our headmaster is a strict ....
   A autocrat   B dictator   C disciplinarian   D authority

2 The doctor warned me that the pills might cause .... effects.
   A secondary   B second   C side   D subsidiary

3 Did you listen to the weather .... this morning?
   A forecast   B prediction   C warning   D foreboding

4 The judge .... the case for an hour.
   A delayed   B dismissed   C postponed   D adjourned

5   Our insurance policy offers immediate .... against the risk of burglary, accident or damage by fire.
    A security   B cover   C care   D relief

6   I'm sorry I'm late. I was .... in the traffic.
    A held in   B held over   C held up   D held down

7   The Leader of the Opposition has appointed Mr Barnaby as .... Minister for Foreign Affairs.
    A ghost   B shadow   C phantom   D fantasy

8   Every word processor we sell comes with a two-year ....
    A assurance   B safeguard   C security   D guarantee

9   I don't .... like the idea of walking home in the dark.
    A so   B much   C very   D fairly

10 Sorry to .... you, but have you got the key to the storeroom?
    A annoy   B bother   C disrupt   D inconvenience

11 Production of the new car has been .... up to meet the increased demand.
    A pulled   B turned   C played   D stepped

12 The Wildlife Society have declared the whale an .... species.
    A extinct   B extinguishing   C endangered   D exhausted

13 Six people were overcome by .... from a container in the laboratory.
    A leaks   B fumes   C outflows   D odours

14 The fire was caused by .... electrical wiring.
    A faulty   B mistaken   C invalid   D withered

15 The Government is .... the danger of lead pollution in our cities.
    A taking stock   B counting up   C looking into   D taking measures

16 The Anti-Nuclear League is holding a .... in Hyde Park on Sunday afternoon.
    A conference   B rally   C seminar   D walk

17 Tickets booked on this flight are not ....
    A transferrable   B moveable   C passable   D assignable

18 The tap was dripping because it needed a new ....
    A wringer   B stopper   C rubber   D washer

19 The outbreak of whooping cough among children under 5 has now reached .... proportions.
   A endemic   B pathological   C epidemic   D contagious

20 The .... of his death were highly suspicious.
   A circumstances   B events   C conditions   D indications

21 Three hundred workers in the steel corporation have been made ....
   A superfluous   B useless   C supernumerary   D redundant

22 The information was .... to the press before it was officially announced.
   A dropped   B leaked   C dripped   D seeped

23 At the memorial service, the priest paid .... to the professor's outstanding contribution to medical science.
   A recognition   B homage   C tribute   D acknowledgement

24 I think the performance of this new car is considerably ....
   A overstated   B overprized   C overcalculated   D overrated

25 The degree of poverty .... to the expected standard of living.
   A compares   B relates   C accords   D depends

SECTION B

*In this section you will find after each of the passages a number of questions or unfinished statements about the passage, each with four suggested answers or ways of finishing. You must choose the one which you think fits best. Underline the letter A, B, C or D against the number of each item, 26 to 40, for the answer you choose. **Give one answer only** to each question. Read each passage right through before choosing your answers.*

FIRST PASSAGE

It would seem that with the rapid pace of modern life and the increased use of technology, persons in administrative positions—businessmen, bureaucrats and the like—are incorporating more and more of what might be described as 'words of convenience' into the English language. These are generally long words, incorporating several ideas, not to say syllables, in one. To the layman, unversed in the complexities of these terms, at best the meaning remains obscure, at worst, it presents all the problems of a foreign language. Conversely, the habit also seems to have arisen of using a phrase of three or four words instead of one, for example 'at this moment in time' rather than 'now'. The reason for this is not clear. Perhaps officials feel that expressions of this kind add importance to otherwise uninteresting facts.

However, it has recently been reported that the Commerce Secretary in President

Reagan's Administration, with the help of a computer system, has launched a crusade against the misuse of English by officials in his department. His aim is to ban the use of multisyllabic jargon and verbal distortion. His message: 'Just use plain, simple English'. He has compiled a 'hit-list' which has been fed into the department computer. Whenever the computer detects a grammatical error or any other kind of linguistic horror, it flashes a message saying 'Don't use this word'. Among the Commerce Secretary's particular dislikes are expressions such as 'prior to' (the computer says use 'before'), 'bottom line', 'more importantly', 'mutually beneficial' and 'contingent upon'.

He feels, with some justification, that the misuse of English, particularly in government positions, often results in lack of communication. He gives as an example a conversation which a former Secretary of State had with one of his aides.

The aide asked for an increase. He was told, 'Because of the fluctuational predisposition of your position's productive capacity as juxtaposed to government standards, it would be momentarily injudicious to advocate an increment.'

When the bewildered aide said, 'I don't get it', he received the reply, 'That's right'.

26 The English used by officials today may

    A   be classed as a language of its own.

    B   require instant transcription.

    C   be totally incomprehensible.

    D   confine itself to technological terms.

27 The aim of the Commerce Secretary's campaign is to

    A   reassess the English language.

    B   clarify the meaning of common words.

    C   encourage people to mean what they say.

    D   simplify forms of expression.

28 The 'hit-list' refers to words or expressions which in the Commerce Secretary's opinion

    A   have unpleasant connotations.

    B   are essentially multi-lingual.

    C   are totally unacceptable.

    D   cannot be computer programmed.

29 'Because of the fluctuational predisposition of your position's productive capacity . . .'
Which of the following expresses the meaning more simply?

    A   We don't like the way you work.

B Your books don't balance.

C You're dishonest.

D You're uninterested in your work.

30 Why did the aide say 'I don't get it'?

    A He realised he wasn't going to get a rise.

    B He didn't understand what had been said to him.

    C He didn't think his request had been understood.

    D He thought he was getting the sack.

SECOND PASSAGE

In our family, as I have told, we lived an isolated life. No friend ever came to the house. Father always said he had no time for people. We had to ask permission to see our friends and that was rarely given; and, if it was, we had to dress up in our best clothes. 'Is your own family not good enough for you?' was the piercing question. My earliest pleasure was therefore in being alone; and to be alone in Paris, knowing nobody, was an intoxication; it was like being on the dizzy brink of knowing everybody. I felt I was drinking the lights of the city and the words I heard spoken by passers-by . . .

    I walked to the Place de la Concorde and there by the bridge in the shade of the warm trees looked over the stone wall into the river. I was instantly under a spell. The water looked still, yet it rustled like a dress. I had never seen water and stone in such pleasant conversation, the stone moonish, shading to saffron like the cheese of Brie, the water womanish and velvet. My solemn young eyes were seeing order and feeling united. I was so moved that I could feel myself grow into a new being. I repeated to myself my vow—for I was at the vowing age—never to leave France and I was so entranced that tears came to my eyes. I walked from bridge to bridge along the Seine, past the acacias, the poplars and the planes that leaned with a graceful precision over the water, each tree like the stroke of a painter's brush. The orderliness of the trees, the gravely spaced avenues, rearranged my mind. My English feeling was for Wordsworthian nature; here nature had been civilised. I was shocked and converted in an hour and though later in life I have often lapsed, the conversion has remained.

31 Being alone in Paris did not worry the writer because he

    A had had a lonely childhood.

    B had been allowed no friends as a child.

    C had learnt to enjoy his own company.

    D had never been to the city before.

32 What enchanted him when he looked over the wall into the river?

    A   The soft sound of the water lapping the wall.

    B   The harmony of stone and water.

    C   The moonlike shape of the wall.

    D   The gentle contours of the water.

33 The scene impressed him so much that he felt he

    A   was in another world.

    B   was unable to move.

    C   had been reborn.

    D   would burst into tears.

34 The writer was totally unprepared for what he saw because he

    A   had never seen nature in the wild.

    B   had a misconception of natural beauty.

    C   had little knowledge of art.

    D   had a preconception of beauty in nature.

35 For the first time the writer realised

    A   the changing beauty of nature.

    B   the effect of order on nature.

    C   the precision of natural beauty.

    D   the orderliness of nature.

THIRD PASSAGE

Extract 1

Brighton and Hove

In 1750 a certain Dr Richard Russell prescribed sea-bathing (and drinking a pint and a half of sea water) as a cure for glandular diseases, and thus, incredibly, started a fashionable trend that brought royalty and artisan alike to Brighton and Hove.

But these twin towns are not simply the grand old ladies of the English seaside. A population of over a quarter of a million, and visitors all the year round, find here a hugely varied and contrasting scene, from boisterous Brighton to elegant Regency Hove.

Brighton's Old Town draws millions of visitors every year. The 'Lanes' are a criss-cross of narrow, red brick-paved alleyways, safe from the noise of traffic, in which are clustered a fascinating collection of antique shops, pubs and cafés.

So whether you are a holidaymaker, conference delegate or student of English, Brighton and Hove will delight you.

Extract 2

The Royal Pavilion, King George's oriental fantasy

Much of the rich history of Brighton and Hove stems from that handsome, wayward, gifted, spendthrift character, George, Prince of Wales (later Prince Regent and finally King George IV). The Prince first visited Brighton in 1783, and by 1822 his Royal Pavilion was completed in the style of the Moghul palaces of India—the most bizarre and exotic palace in Europe.

The Pavilion, open to the public every day, is fully furnished in its original style, including furniture on permanent loan from our present Queen.

Of the same era, many fine examples of more conventional Regency and early Victorian planning delight the eye elsewhere—notable are Lewes Crescent in Brighton and Adelaide Crescent in Hove both proudly facing the sea.

Extract 3

Preston Manor (2 miles/3 kms) with its original 17th-, 18th- and 19th-century English furnishings gives a charming glimpse of the life of an English country gentleman. It has a delightful walled period garden. Open Weds to Suns all year. Tel: 603005.

Extract 4

Fishbourne Roman Palace & Museum, Salthill Rd, Fishbourne, Nr Chichester (30 miles/48 kms away). One wing of a magnificent 1st Century Palace displayed inside modern cover building with many fine mosaic floors. Replica dining room, site museum, audio-visual programme, restored Roman Garden. Cafeteria, picnic area, free parking. Open daily March—Nov. Tel: 0243 785859.

36 In extract 1 the origin of Brighton's popularity is attributed to

    A drinking sea water.

    B a craze of sea-bathing.

    C medical advice.

    D royal patronage.

37 In extract 2 the Royal Pavilion is referred to as an 'oriental fantasy' because it

    A was built by an Eastern prince.

    B resembles an Indian temple.

    C was brought from the Far East.

    D is extravagantly designed.

38 Preston Manor, referred to in extract 3,

    A has been refurnished in the original style.

    B contains examples of English craftsmanship.

C   is typical of present-day England.

D   is the home of an English gentleman.

39 Unlike the buildings described in extracts 2 and 3, the Roman Palace at Fishbourne is

A   prehistoric.

B   a replica.

C   incomplete.

D   a museum.

40 The information in these extracts probably comes from a

A   local directory.

B   tourist handout.

C   textbook.

D   historical survey.

PAPER 2 COMPOSITION (2 hours)

*Write **two only** of the following composition exercises. Your answers must follow exactly the instructions given.*

1   Write a descriptive account of a visit to an exhibition or museum.
    (About 350 words)

2   Write a balanced discussion on the theme 'Power corrupts'. You may write in the form of a dialogue between two speakers, or in essay form. (About 350 words)

3   Discuss the effect that computers may have on employment. (About 200 words)

4   The following headlines appeared in a national newspaper. Write the report that accompanied them. (About 200 words)

    PRESIDENT KANGO ASSASSINATED
    Mangora Islands in revolt
    Take-over by Self-Determination Party
    Islanders jubilant

5   (See Appendix: Prescribed texts)

PAPER 3 USE OF ENGLISH (2 hours)

SECTION A

1 *Fill each of the numbered blanks in the following passage with **one** suitable word.*

I remember a film, I forget what it was .... (1), in which four people were interrogated .... (2) the character and life-style of a woman who had been murdered. All of .... (3) had known her well, but to .... (4) of them she presented a different .... (5). The man who loved her .... (6) her as amusing, intelligent and extravagant. The girl who had been .... (7) school with her said she was reserved, ... (8) to make friends and .... (9) to be mean. Her boss, for whom she worked as a secretary, ... (10) her hardworking but dull, the last person to inspire passion, ... (11) alone murder. Her landlady said she was easy to get on .... (12), untidy and careless about money. 'I always had to .... (13) her about the rent,' she said, 'but I liked her. She was always cheerful and willing to lend a .... (14) if anyone was .... (15) trouble.' The interest of the film was not .... (16) much in who committed the murder, but in .... (17) it showed the way in which we all show different sides of .... (18) to different people. For most of us, this is not a conscious deceit but .... (19) a chameleon-like reaction, a form of self-protection in a world in which our .... (20) of security is constantly threatened.

2 *Finish each of the following sentences in such a way that it means exactly the same as the sentence printed before it.*

EXAMPLE: There are no trains after midnight.

ANSWER: The trains *don't run after midnight.*

a) There were 500 redundancies in that firm this summer.

500 workers ....

b) He predicted a win for the Labour Party in the next general election.

He was sure ....

c) I didn't get the job because I had not had enough practical experience.

If ....

d) To what extent do they agree with our proposals?

How far are ....?

85

e) There have been three reports of sightings of a UFO over London last night.

Three people ....

f) Never underestimate the value of good staff relations.

The value ....

g) He gave a two-hour lecture on aerodynamics.

His lecture ....

h) She doesn't speak Spanish as well as she speaks English.

She speaks ....

3   *Fill each of the numbered blanks with a suitable word or phrase.*

EXAMPLE: I know he lives in London but he *didn't give me his* telephone number.

a) It's rather hot in here.
   Why .... your coat?

b) I've run out of cash. I hope .... a cheque.

c) If we hadn't caught the last bus, we .... home.

d) If you don't mind, I'd .... at home this evening.

e) I .... skiing, but I don't much care for it any more.

f) When I told her what had happened, she .... say.

4   *For each of the sentences below, write a new sentence as similar as possible in meaning to the original sentence, but using the words given: these words must **not be altered** in any way.*

EXAMPLE: Peter inherited the house when his father died.
         left

ANSWER: *Peter's father left the house to him.*

a) He doesn't think much of their marketing methods.
   opinion

   ....

b) There is no difference in the price of these two washing machines.
   same

   ....

86

c) He was dismissed for incompetence.
lost

....

d) There is nothing you can do except agree to his demands.
option

....

e) After the accident, he couldn't see out of one eye.
blind

....

f) I found this book incomprehensible.
word

....

g) They say this picture was painted by Rembrandt.
attributed

....

h) She speaks seven languages fluently.
accomplished

....

SECTION B

5 *Read the following passage, then answer the questions which follow it.*

In writing autobiography, especially one that looks back at childhood, the only truth is what you remember. No one else who was there can agree with you because he has his own version of what he saw. He also holds to a personal truth of himself, based on an indefatigable self-regard. One neighbour's reaction, after reading my book, sums up
5 this double vision: 'You hit off old Tom to the life,' he said, 'but why d'you tell all those lies about me?'
     Seven brothers and sisters shared my early years, and we lived on top of each other. If they had all written of those days, each account would have been different, and each one true. We saw the same events at different heights, at different levels of mood and
10 hunger—one suppressing an incident as too much to bear, another building it large around him, each reflecting one world according to the temper of his day, his age, the chance heat of his blood. Recalling it differently, as we were bound to do, what was it, in fact, we saw? Which one among us has the truth of it now? And which one shall be the judge? The truth is, of course, that there is no pure truth, only the moody
15 accounts of witnesses.

But perhaps the widest pitfall in autobiography is the writer's censorship of self. Unconscious or deliberate, it often releases an image of one who could never have lived. Flat, shadowy, prim and bloodless, it is a leaf pressed dry on the page, the surrogate chosen for public office so that the author might survive in secret.

With a few exceptions, the first person singular is one of the recurrent shams of literature—the faceless 'I', opaque and neuter, fruit of some failure between honesty and nerve. To be fair, one should not confine this failing to literature. One finds it in painting, too, whose centuries of self-portraits, deprecating and tense, are often as alike as brothers. This cipher no doubt is the 'I' of all of us, the only self that our skills can see.

For the writer, after all, it may be a necessary one, the one that works best on the page. An ego that takes up too much of a book can often wither the rest of it. Charles Dickens's narrators were often as dry as wafers, but they compèred Gargantuan worlds. The autobiographer's self can be a transmitter of life that is larger than his own—though it is best that he should be shown taking part in that life and involved in its dirt and splendours. The dead stick 'I', like the staff of the maypole, can be the centre of the turning world, or it can be the electric needle that picks up and relays the thronging choirs of life around it.

a) How does the writer classify memory in writing an autobiography?

....

b) What was his neighbour's reaction to reading the writer's autobiography?

....

c) What do you think the writer means by 'an indefatigable self-regard' (line 4)?

....

d) Why does the writer refer to this reaction as 'double vision' (line 5)?

....

e) Explain the phrase 'on top of each other' (line 7).

....

f) To what period does 'those days' refer in line 8?

....

g) Give two reasons why people might record the same incident differently.

....

....

h) Explain in other words the phrase 'censorship of self' (line 16).

....

i) What words does the writer use to describe the way in which autobiographers frequently present themselves in their books?

....

j) Why does the writer refer to the use of the first person singular as 'the faceless I' (line 21)?

....

k) What do self-portraits have in common with autobiographies?

....

l) In what way can the first person singular act as a transmitter?

....

m) To what does 'its' (line 31) refer?

....

n) Which line in Paragraph 5 best explains why a writer may decide to use the first person singular?

....

o) Summarise in 50—100 words the reasons which support the phrase 'there is no pure truth' (line 14).

....

....

....

....

....

....

....

....

....

PAPER 4 LISTENING COMPREHENSION (Approx. 30 minutes)

FIRST PART

For questions 1—5 fill in the prices on the price list below (some have been filled in for you). For each of the questions 6—8 put a tick (✓) in one of the boxes A, B, C or D.

SEAT PRICES		
Location		**Price**
1 **Stalls**	(front)	
	(row R back)	£24–00
2 **Circle**	(front)	£30–00
	(sides)	
3 **Grand tier**		
4 **Balcony**		
5 **Boxes** (4 seats)		

6 Why doesn't the woman book seats in the balcony?

A They aren't expensive enough.

B Her father isn't supposed to exert himself.

C There aren't four seats together there.

D It is impossible to see the stage clearly.

A	
B	
C	
D	

7 It's important for the family not to be too far away from the stage as they

A need to pay attention to the words.

B want to be able to lipread.

C must listen closely to the music.

D do not know the plot of the opera.

A	
B	
C	
D	

8   Why does the woman order cold suppers to be sent to the box?

    A   There is nowhere else to eat near the opera house.

    B   It is to be a birthday treat for her father.

    C   It will be too late for them to eat elsewhere after the opera.

    D   The opera house bars only serve snacks and drinks.

A	
B	
C	
D	

SECOND PART

For each of the questions 1—4 put a tick (√) in one of the boxes A, B, C or D.

1   Susan has asked Paul to show her how to print because she

    A   wants to be a better photographer.

    B   is interested in photographic techniques.

    C   can't afford to have the prints done in a shop.

    D   wants to develop her own film.

A	
B	
C	
D	

2   Paul tells Susan to pour the developer into a bottle

    A   so that it can mix with the water.

    B   because he hasn't sufficient equipment.

    C   because it speeds up the development time.

    D   to separate it from the fixer.

A	
B	
C	
D	

3   What is the purpose of switching off the light?

    A   It prevents the photographic paper being damaged.

    B   It gives Paul some relief from the blinding glare.

    C   It stops the negatives from becoming dull.

    D   It allows them to use the safelamp.

A	
B	
C	
D	

4   In the end Susan feels that printing is

    A   very difficult.

    B   fairly simple.

    C   rather tricky.

    D   pretty uninteresting.

A	
B	
C	
D	

THIRD PART

For each of the questions 1—4 put a tick (√) in one of the boxes A, B, C or D.

1 Giorgio won't have to pay tax on a new car in Britain if he

   A has driven it for more than a year.

   B exports it within twelve months.

   C sells it back to the dealer within a year.

   D keeps it in Britain for more than a year.

A	
B	
C	
D	

2 An MOT certificate is required for all cars

   A imported into the UK.

   B manufactured abroad.

   C of a certain age.

   D in need of servicing.

A	
B	
C	
D	

3 The date that a car was first in use is recorded on the

   A logbook.

   B driving licence.

   C numberplates.

   D tax disc.

A	
B	
C	
D	

4 In the UK an international driving licence is

   A only valid for six months.

   B subject to annual review.

   C equivalent to a British one.

   D subject to conditions.

A	
B	
C	
D	

FOURTH PART

For each of the questions 1—4 put a tick (✓) in one of the boxes A, B, C or D.

1 Who is making the announcement?

A Air Traffic Control.

B A station announcer.

C A tour operator.

D An airline official.

A	
B	
C	
D	

2 The flight has been cancelled owing to

A metal fatigue.

B a mechanical fault.

C a power cut.

D a technicians' strike.

A	
B	
C	
D	

3 Passengers who have not yet checked in for flight 507 should

A leave their luggage in the main hall.

B wait for further information.

C contact the airline enquiry desk.

D go to the Silver Wings lounge.

A	
B	
C	
D	

4 Special provision has been made for the comfort of

A families with young children.

B the physically handicapped.

C school parties.

D stand-by passengers.

A	
B	
C	
D	

PAPER 5 INTERVIEW (Approx. 20 minutes)

(i) *Look at this picture carefully and be prepared to answer some questions about it.*

1   What are these men doing?

2   Where are they?

3   What is the purpose of the ladder?

4   Does the situation seem dangerous?

Mountaineering
Dangerous sports
Man's need to take risks and explore

(ii)   *Look at this passage and be prepared to answer some questions about it and then to read it aloud.*

Before the staff meeting closes, I'm sure all my teaching colleagues will be interested to know that the Southern Counties Educational Computer Conference, sponsored by Radar Electronics, will be held at this college from February 16—18. The first two days will concentrate on the use of the computer as a teaching aid across the curriculum. The learning problems of multi-ethnic, multi-linguistic groups will be a prime consideration. On the last day you'll be invited to take part in an open discussion on the adult approach to computer awareness.

SAMPLE QUESTIONS

Who do you think the speaker is talking to?
Where is the conference going to take place?
What is the purpose of the conference?
What problems will be discussed?

Now read the passage aloud.

(iii)   *There may be a variety of options offered in this section. Choose one of the following:*

a)   Discussion.

Be prepared to discuss a subject initiated by the examiner, for example:
The role of the police in society

You may be invited to give your comments on various aspects, such as:
   whether or not the police should be armed
   crowd control in demonstrations
   police brutality

If you are participating in a group discussion you might be asked to speak individually about one of these categories.

b) Consider these two statements:

No spiders are insects.
All tarantulas are spiders.

Now say which of these answers is a logical conclusion to the statements:

A   No spiders are tarantulas.
B   All tarantulas are insects.
C   All spiders are tarantulas.
D   No tarantulas are insects.

(Explain your reasoning to your group/the examiner.)

c) Prescribed texts—See Appendix.

Appendix: Prescribed Texts

Candidates may choose one of the questions on prescribed books as a basis for one topic in Paper 2 (Composition) and one for the Paper 5 (Interview). The texts set for 1985 are:

MARGARET DRABBLE: *The Millstone*
GEORGE ELIOT: *Silas Marner*
ROBERT GRAVES: *Goodbye To All That*

Different texts may be substituted from year to year for one or all of the books prescribed.

Candidates should be reminded that only **one** of these topics can be chosen for Paper 2 (Composition). The other must be selected from topics 1—4.

Following are examples of the kind of topic the candidate may be asked to deal with on prescribed books:

THE MILLSTONE

COMPOSITION (Paper 2)

a) 'My career has always been marked by a strange mixture of confidence and cowardice . . .'
Comment on this statement by Rosmund in relation to her pregnancy.

b) What insight does the book give into the problems of the single parent today? Discuss.

c) Write an account of Rosmund's first visit to the ante-natal clinic and her impressions.

INTERVIEW (Paper 5)

a) What was Rosmund's lifestyle before she became pregnant?

b) Who was Lydia? What part does she play in the story?

c) What happened when Rosmund finally met George after the birth of her baby?

SILAS MARNER

COMPOSITION (Paper 2)

a) Compare the social attitudes of Dolly Winthrop and Nancy Lammeter.

b) 'Everything comes to light Nancy, sooner or later. When God Almighty wills it, our secrets are found out. I've lived with a secret on my mind, but I'll keep it from you no longer ...'
What caused Godfrey to make this statement and what were the consequences?

c) What do we learn from *Silas Marner* about life in an English village in the mid-nineteenth century?

INTERVIEW (Paper 5)

a) What was the reaction in the Rainbow Inn when Silas reported the theft of his money?

b) What terrible event occurred while the guests were enjoying themselves at the Red House New Year party?

c) 'It had been his companion for twelve years, always standing in the same spot, always lending its handle to him in the early morning ...'
To what incident does this refer? What does it tell us about Silas?

GOODBYE TO ALL THAT

COMPOSITION (Paper 2)

a) In what ways do you think the experiences of a soldier in combat today would differ from those of those of Robert Graves? Discuss.

b) What difficulties did Robert Graves find in adapting to peacetime life in England?

c) 'I was both more consistent and less heroic than Siegfried (Sassoon) ...'
Comment.

INTERVIEW (Paper 5)

a) What were Robert Graves' first impression of the frontline trenches?

b) Describe Robert Graves' first meeting with Colonel T. E. Lawrence.

c) What do you learn from the book about Robert Graves' schooldays at Charterhouse?